Getty-Dubay®
ITALIC HANDWRITING SERIES

INSTRUCTION MANUAL
Basic & Cursive Italic

International Edition

by
Barbara Getty & Inga Dubay

Handwriting Success™
Portland, Oregon USA

GETTY-DUBAY® ITALIC HANDWRITING SERIES

BOOK A · Basic Italic
14 mm body height

BOOK B · Basic Italic
11 mm, 9mm body height

BOOK C · Basic Italic
9 mm, 6 mm body height   Introduction to Cursive Italic

BOOK D · Cursive Italic
6 mm, 5mm body height   Includes Basic Italic

BOOK E · Cursive Italic
6 mm, 5mm body height   Includes Basic Italic

BOOK F · Cursive Italic
6 mm, 5mm, 4mm body height   Includes Basic Italic

BOOK G · Cursive Italic
5 mm, 4mm body height   Includes Basic Italic

INSTRUCTION MANUAL

INTERNATIONAL EDITION
Copyright 2009, 2013 by Barbara M. Getty and Inga S. Dubay
ISBN 978-1-7334352-1-5

FOURTH EDITION
Copyright 2009, 2013 by Barbara M. Getty and Inga S. Dubay
THIRD EDITION
Copyright 1994 by Barbara M. Getty and Inga S. Dubay
SECOND EDITION
Copyright 1986 by Barbara M. Getty and Inga S. Dubay
REVISED EDITION
Copyright 1980 by Barbara M. Getty and Inga S. Dubay
FIRST EDITION
Copyright 1979 by Barbara M. Getty and Inga S. Dubay

All rights reserved.
This text may not be reproduced in whole or in part
without the express written permission of the copyright holder.
Getty-Dubay® is a registered trademark of Handwriting Success, LLC in the United States of America.

Published by Handwriting Success, LLC
Portland, Oregon USA
www.handwritingsuccess.com

Printed in various locations around the world via Ingram.

Cover Design: Sinda Markham and Jonathan Dubay
Front cover picture: Barn near Dufur, Oregon
Back cover pictures: Chicory flowers, Prong-horned Antelope

CONTENTS

- Introduction 1
- About Italic and the Series 2
- Comparison of handwriting 4
- Basic and cursive alphabets 5
- Components of the *Series* 6–8

Teaching Getty-Dubay® Italic Handwriting
- Teaching Italic in the Elementary Classroom .. 10–12
- The beginning writer 13
- Process, letter dimensions, assessment ... 14–15
- Special concerns 16–17
- Notes to teachers
  - Book A 18–19
  - Book B 20–21
  - Book C 22–23
  - Book D 24–25
  - Book E 26–27
  - Book F 28–29
  - Book G 30–31
- Letter descriptions
  - Family 1   *i · j · l* 32–33
  - Family 2   *k · v · w · x · z* 34–35
  - Families 3 & 4   *h · m · n · r & u · y* 36–37
  - Families 5 & 6   *a · d · g · q & b · p* 38–39
  - Families 7 & 8   *o · e · c · s & f · t* 40–41
  - Basic italic capitals 42
  - Cursive capitals 43
- Numerals 44
- Cursive join descriptions
  - Transition to cursive italic 45
  - Joins 1 & 2 46
  - Joins 3 & 4 47
  - Joins 5 & 6 48
  - Joins 7 & 8 & lifts 49
- Reading looped cursive 50–51
- Sequence of skills 52

Getty-Dubay® Italic Handwriting Assessment
- Assessment 54–55
- Letter dimensions
  - Options 56
  - Shape guidelines 57
  - Size guidelines 58
- Slope guidelines 59
- Spacing & speed guidelines 60
- Timed writing 61
- Assessment questions
  - Basic italic lowercase 62–63
  - Basic italic capitals 64
  - Cursive capitals 65
  - Cursive lowercase joins 66
- Assessment chart 67
- Self-assessment in handwriting 68

Getty-Dubay® Italic Handwriting Implementation
- Implementing Italic Handwriting Series 70–71
- Sample letter to parents 72
- Inservice
  - Two-hour inservice outline 73
  - Basic & cursive lowercase 74
  - Cursive italic lowercase joins 75
  - Basic & cursive italic capitals 76

Getty-Dubay® Activities/Supplements
- Handwriting activities & projects 78–79
- Ways to use Italic 80
- Letter booklet 81
- Simple handsewn book 82
- Accordion book 83
- Spiral writing 84
- Pop-ups 85
- Development of the alphabet 86–93
- Glossary 94
- Bibliography 95–96

Getty-Dubay® Italic Handwriting Series Ruled Lines
- 9mm (horizontal format) 98
- 9mm 99
- 6mm 100–101
- 6mm with capital line 102
- 5mm with capital line 103
- 4mm with capital line 104
- 9mm letter lines (horizontal format) .. 105
- 6mm letter lines 106
- 5mm letter lines 107
- Envelope pattern 108

ABOUT THE AUTHORS

BARBARA GETTY, B.A., M.A.T., was an adjunct professor at Portland Community College where she taught calligraphy and handwriting from 1969 to 1999. She was an elementary school teacher for fourteen years and taught at Portland State University and Lewis and Clark College in Portland, Oregon. She received her undergraduate degree at Lewis and Clark College, did graduate work at Portland State University, and earned a Master of Arts in Teaching degree from Lewis and Clark College. Her work has appeared in many publications including *International Calligraphy Today*.

Authors Inga Dubay and Barbara Getty

INGA DUBAY, B.A., was an adjunct professor at the Oregon College of Art & Craft in Portland, Oregon where she taught for 25 years. She was head of the Book Arts Department at the college for six years and also taught at Portland State University for eight years. She began teaching handwriting to children in 1969. She studied at Mills College, received her B.A. from the University of Oregon, and did graduate work at the Art Academy in Oslo, Norway. Her work has appeared in numerous publications including *Calligraphy Review*, *Letter Arts Review* and *Lettering Arts*.

BOTH AUTHORS studied with Oregon Calligrapher Laureate Lloyd Reynolds and have exhibited their work nationally and internationally. They are co-authors of the *Getty-Dubay® Italic Handwriting Series, Write Now: The Getty-Dubay® Program for Handwriting Success, Getty-Dubay® Italic Calligraphy for School & Home, Italic Letters: Calligraphy & Handwriting* and the DVD *Write Now! Getty-Dubay® Italic Handwriting*. They have conducted workshops nationally and internationally including 170 seminars for medical professionals and patient safety conferences in Florence, Italy and at the World Health Organization in Copenhagen, Denmark. Their work has been featured in numerous publications including *American Hospital Association Trustee Magazine, American Medical News, Cardiology Today, Martha Stewart Living, Medical Economics, Men's Health, Time,* and *U.S. News & World Report*. They have also been featured on ABC, CBS, CNN, NBC, NPR, PBS and in newspapers across the country, including *The Boston Globe, The Houston Chronicle, The Los Angeles Times, The New York Times, The San Francisco Chronicle, The Wall Street Journal,* and *The Washington Post*.

ACKNOWLEDGMENTS

Our approach to italic handwriting is influenced by the writings and teachings of Lloyd J. Reynolds.

We would like to acknowledge the following authors for their contribution to today's interest in italic handwriting: Kerstin Anckers, Nan Jay Barchowsky, Gunnlaugur S E Briem, Fred Eager, Alfred Fairbank, Tom Gourdie, Christopher Jarman, Charles Lehman, Rosemary Sassoon, Jacqueline Svaren, Wolf Von Eckardt and Irene Wellington.

We appreciate Mark Van Stone for generously sharing his knowledge of the Roman alphabet.

We want to thank the following people for help, support and encouragement: Dr. Carol Burden, Dr. Larry Burden, Mike Carstensen, members of the Edmonton Calligraphic Society, Kate Gladstone, Cherie Chichester Glasse, Mary Cooper, Betty Jo Cramer, June Gaps, Joyce Gilham, Mary Goldmanner, Emily Foster, Dr. Eric Kimmel, Kim McDodge, Mike Mitchel, Linda Neigebauer Sellers, Nancy Borquist Olson, Ben Paroulek, Jean Phelps, Ed Robinson, Carolyn Sheldon, Ann Shipstead, Fran Sloan, Mickey Templeton, Melicent Whinston, Mike Wong and Marilyn Zornado.

A special thanks to the students and teachers who first piloted our program in 1979 at Aloha Park, Bethany, Catlin Gabel, Metropolitan Learning Center, Patterson, Sabin, and Terra Linda schools.

We want to thank Kris Holmes and Charles Bigelow for creating the Lucida Sans School Italic font especially for the third edition of the *Getty-Dubay Italic Handwriting Series*.

Our thanks to Vicki Swartz and Tia Wulff for their inspiration and ideas about the teaching and assessment of italic handwriting in the elementary classroom. Their personal statements are found on pages 10 and 68.

We are especially grateful to Charlie Blank, Kay Fujita, Olive Hilton, Mackenzie Jeans, Mary Laughlin, Marilyn Manchester, Tony Midson, Laurie Mitchell, Thom Perry, and Tena Spears for thier assistance and support.

We want to thank our families: Todd Getty, Joseph Dubay, Christopher Dubay, Gregory Dubay, and Jonathan Dubay as well as our parents, Peter Pfau and Vera Pfau Miller, and Helge and Olive Shipstead.

We have greatly appreciated each other's mutual support, encouragement, and inspiration.

Barbara M. Getty & Inga S. Dubay
Portland, Oregon

INTRODUCTION

abcdefghijklmnopqrstuvwxyz

Handwriting is a necessity in many areas of everyday life. Computers are an integral part of most school programs and most of the words we read today are created by machine. Nevertheless, children are required to use handwriting daily at school, and most literate adults use pen or pencil on a daily basis in their work and in their personal lives.

The authors believe that handwriting will persist in everyday use for two simple reasons—it is convenient and, above all, it is personal. However, because handwriting in the USA is generally so poor, we have become a "please print" nation—invariably being asked to print rather than use cursive (joined letters) in situations where legibility is important. The U. S. Postal Service routes 38 million pieces of mail with illegible addresses to its dead letter office every year at a cost of several million dollars. Business losses due to illegible handwriting (handwritten instructions, bookkeeping figures, addresses, etc.) amount to many millions of dollars a year.

Conventional Instruction

Until the turn of the 20th century, handwriting was a major discipline in the classroom. In American schools, the general practice has been to introduce young students to a drawn manuscript alphabet known as "ball and stick." This alphabet demands exceptional motor coordination in order for the student to form circles and straight lines. A cumbersome series of strokes is required to form many of the letters, ignoring rhythmic movement—the essential nature of handwriting.

As students are just beginning to gain some mastery of these forms, usually at the latter part of second grade or the beginning of third, they are asked to abandon their new skill and learn to write a different set of 52 letters known as *"looped cursive."* This is frustrating and confusing to many learners.

Paradoxically, the *looped cursive* that is generally taught in upper grades stems from letterforms inscribed by copperplate engravers and not from letters designed for handwriting. When these forms were taught as a major subject with hours of practice, an elegant hand could be the reward.

However, today, school systems are increasingly reluctant to devote much time to direct instruction in handwriting, except in the early grades, and most teacher-training programs barely present it or ignore it altogether.

The *Getty-Dubay® Italic Handwriting Series*, with its emphasis on continuity of instruction, legibility, and ease of mastery, resolves many of these issues.

abcdefghijklmnopqrstuvwxyz

ABOUT ITALIC & THE GETTY-DUBAY® ITALIC HANDWRITING SERIES

Italic is a modern handwriting system based on enduring classic letterforms that first developed in Italy and were later used in England and Europe. Contemporary italic presents one simple lowercase alphabet that is cursive in nature—the letters are based on an elliptical shape conforming to natural hand movements and require few lifts of the writing instrument. These letterforms assist the natural, rhythmic movement of the hand during writing and fulfill the need for both legibility and speed.

Basic and Cursive Italic

The *Getty-Dubay® Italic Handwriting Series* letterforms consist of an unjoined set of letters, presented in the first three books (BOOKS A, B, and C), and briefly as review in the rest of the series (BOOKS D, E, F, & G).

A quick brown fox jumps over the lazy dog.

At the end of BOOK C, entrance and exit strokes (serifs) are added to facilitate joining the letters for cursive.

A quick brown fox jumps over the lazy dog.

Throughout the student's educational experience no major changes occur in the basic letterforms.

The contrast in the series of strokes required to write four italic letters and four **"ball and stick"** manuscript letters used in primary grades is shown below. In each case, the italic is written in one stroke while the manuscript letter is formed in two or three strokes.

a b h m   easily written single-stroke letters
lowercase basic italic

a b h m   multi-stroke letters requiring several lifts
manuscript: "ball and stick"

The only transitions in the *Getty-Dubay® Italic Handwriting Series* are the addition of serifs, and diagonal and horizontal joins for the cursive.

handwriting becomes *handwriting*

However, when children learn *looped cursive*, they are confronted with 52 virtually new letterforms to master. The further addition of awkward joins frustrates the learner and promotes illegibility.

handwriting becomes *handwriting*

Italic capital letters are very similar to those of the traditional manuscript alphabet. These capitals retain the same basic forms throughout the grades, except for optional flourishes which may be added in BOOK D and beyond.

F becomes F • G becomes G or G • S remains S

However, many *looped cursive* capitals are confusing and complicated to the eight- or nine-year-old and to older students learning English. Note the changes from the printed capitals to the looped cursive capitals below:

F 𝓕   G 𝓖   S 𝓢

Note how similar are the italic basic and cursive capitals:

A B C D E F G H   BASIC ITALIC
A B C D E F G H   CURSIVE ITALIC

One of the outstanding features of the Getty-Dubay Italic Handwriting Series is that it provides a smooth transition from the print script basic italic to cursive italic.

The fundamental assessment procedure of LOOK, PLAN, PRACTICE is built into the *Series* throughout the student workbooks. Assessment, by the student and teacher, is an integral part of this program.

Regardless of how much or how little handwriting is done in adult life, legible letters are still fundamental in education. Italic equips the learner with a legible script. Recognizing the need for a stronger handwriting program, many schools throughout the nation are adopting the *Getty-Dubay® Italic Handwriting Series*.

A Doctor Comments on Italic

"I have been using italic as my ordinary handwriting since 1974. There are many reasons. First of all is that its clarity and ease of legibility make it easy for other health professionals such as nurses and pharmacists to interpret what I write without error.

"I also enjoy the aesthetic aspect of interjecting some art into my everyday work. As I and others look through the huge quantity of unreadable medical records, I always feel profoundly thankful when someone has had the respect and common sense to write clearly. There is yet another, more subtle influence that this remarkable script exerts, and that is upon the writer himself or herself. When the physician consciously chooses to communicate thought clearly, it forces one to think more clearly and this in turn fosters greater mental discipline and organization.

"All of these purposes and many more operate each time I uncap my pen. I believe that all of this ultimately benefits the patients with whom I work in that good medical care requires a very large dose of clarity of thought and purpose melded with compassion and art.

"Long live legibility!"

Paul O. Jacobs, MD

COMPARISON OF FIVE HANDWRITING PROGRAMS

This is a comparative analysis of the letterforms of five commonly used handwriting programs. Both capital and lowercase letters are shown in the following chart. The number of letter shape and letter slope changes from manuscript to cursive in each program is documented below.

The GETTY-DUBAY® ITALIC HANDWRITING SERIES uses an elliptical shape for lowercase letters which conforms to natural hand movement and requires very few pencil lifts. Manuscript lowercase letters of the "ball and stick" form require many pencil lifts and circular shapes which can be difficult for the beginning writer.

Getty-Dubay® basic italic uses manuscript lowercase letters without serifs added to the basic letter, providing a completely sans serif (no serif) printed form of writing for the beginner. D'Nealian uses serifs on ten manuscript lowercase letters, resulting in the beginning writer never learns a sans serif manuscript.

During the transition from manuscript to cursive (end of second grade and/or beginning of third grade), most handwriting programs require a traumatic relearning of lowercase and capital letter shapes. The GETTY-DUBAY® ITALIC HANDWRITING SERIES provides a smooth transition from manuscript to cursive as only one capital letter (Y) changes shape. The Getty-Dubay® program builds on previously learned concepts as the manuscript lowercase letters are simply joined for cursive. Other programs require the relearning of all or many letter shapes during the transition from manuscript to cursive.

The Getty-Dubay® program uses no loops, providing an uncomplicated cursive and thereby aiding legibility. In the other programs, the use of long looped ascenders and descenders in lowercase letters and looped serifs in capital letters are detrimental to legibility. (This is why we are a "Please Print" world.) Getty-Dubay® cursive capitals are logically based on the manuscript capitals. The cursive capitals used by Palmer, Zaner-Bloser, D'Nealian and Handwriting Without Tears often bear little resemblance to the manuscript capitals.

In the Getty-Dubay® program, capital height to body height is the same as the fonts used in most books and on computers. The size of capitals, ascenders and descenders allows closer writing lines without tangling descenders with ascenders, thereby improving legibility.

The 5° letter slope of Getty-Dubay® remains consistent in manuscript and cursive. This is a natural slope which is comfortable for the beginning writer. Palmer and Zaner-Bloser require a dramatic change from 0° in manuscript to 27° in cursive besides the relearning of 52 new letter shapes. In D'Nealian, both manuscript and cursive use a 17° slope — generally too sloped for the beginning writer.

The GETTY-DUBAY ITALIC HANDWRITING SERIES provides the easiest transition from manuscript to cursive with the fewest letter shape changes and the easiest consistent slope. The Getty-Dubay program also produces handwriting that is both legible and aesthetically pleasing.

HANDWRITING PROGRAM	CHANGE FROM MANUSCRIPT TO CURSIVE		Slope Change
	Shape Change		
	Capitals	Lowercase	
Italic	1	0	None (all 5°)
Palmer	26	26	0° to 30°
Zaner-Bloser	26	22	0° to 30°
D'Nealian	18	13	None (all 17°)
HWT	15	15	None (all 0°)

THE TRANSITION FROM BASIC TO CURSIVE IN COMMON HANDWRITING METHODS.

COMPONENTS OF THE GETTY-DUBAY® ITALIC HANDWRITING SERIES
www.handwritingsuccess.com

The core component of the *Getty-Dubay® Italic Handwriting Series* is a set of seven student workbooks A through G.

A note about grades.
Because students normally develop at different rates, the authors are reluctant to assign rigid expectations regarding the appropriate workbooks for particular grade levels. The determination of which book is appropriate for a student should be decided by the teacher in each case. The following levels are a guide.

BOOK A - (Kindergarten) is recommended for kindergarten, pre-school, or early first grade. Basic italic capital letters are presented one letter to a page, 52 pages. Each of these pages also contains an illustration and an accompanying word or words for the student to trace and copy. Numerals and basic writing patterns are also included. Illustrated.
11" x 8 ½" format. 14 mm body height. 72 pp.

BOOK B - (1st grade) is recommended for first grade, late kindergarten, or early second grade. The format is the same as that of Book A. Lowercase and capital letters are presented one letter to a page (52). A word or words, short sentences and illustrations are included on each page. The vocabulary emphasis is on words with short vowels. Some long vowel words, words with digraphs, sight words and numerals are also included. Illustrated.
11" x 8 ½" format. 11– 9mm body height. 64 pp.

BOOK C - (2nd grade) is recommended for second grade, the latter part of first grade, or third grade. The basic italic lowercase, capitals and numerals are reviewed through the use of words and sentences. Writing practice includes modes of transportation A through Z, days of the week, months of the year and sentences. The entrance and exit strokes are added to the basic lowercase letters in preparation for the cursive joins. The first five cursive italic joins are introduced. Illustrated.
8 ½" x 11". 9mm–6mm body height. 68 pp.

BOOK D - (3rd grade) is recommended for third grade or the latter part of second grade. Basic italic lowercase and capitals are reviewed together, including twelve rules of capitalization and uses of basic italic. Writing practice uses names of people, haiku, acrostic, cinquain, limerick, formula poems, tongue twisters, and couplets. Also included are: vowel sounds, consonant sounds, homophones, homographs, phonograms, prefixes and suffixes. The introduction of the cursive capitals includes an historical development of each letter. Numerals and numeral words are also presented. A letter and envelope instruction page is included. Illustrated.
8 ½" x 11" format. 6mm–5mm body height. 88 pp.

BOOK E - (4 th grade) is recommended for fourth grade or the latter part of third grade. Basic italic lowercase, capitals, and numerals are reviewed as well as use of basic italic. Practice of cursive joins includes words using vowel sounds, consonant sounds, phonograms, prefixes, suffixes, and other letter combinations. Sentence content includes the five kingdoms of life, DNA, animal groups, minerals, vegetation zones/biomes, our solar system, and galaxies. Cursive capital practice includes origins of our alphabet and cities of the world. Instruction includes slope guidelines, timed writing, practice reading looped cursive, and letter/booklet/envelope production. Illustrated.
8 ½" x 11" format. 5mm-4mm body height. 64pp.

BOOK F - (5th grade) is recommended for fifth grade or the latter part of 4th grade, or early sixth grade. The basic italic letter forms and numerals are reviewed. Practice of cursive joins includes words using vowel sounds, consonant sounds, prefixes, suffixes, and abbreviations. Writing practice includes words, such as homophones, synonyms, and antonyms; word origins, such as compound words, portmanteau words, acronyms, and onomatopoeia; word groups, such as analogies, similes, metaphors, oxymora and euphemisms, and word entertainment such as palindromes, rebuses, and Tom Swifties. Historical development of the alphabet is included. Illustrated.
8 ½" x 11" format. 6mm–5mm–4mm body height. 64 pp.

Components of the Getty-Dubay® Italic Handwriting Series

BOOK G - (6th-8th grade and adult) is recommended for later fifth grade, sixth to eighth grade and adult. The development of both a "printing" or unjoined form of writing (basic italic) and a cursive or joined form of writing (cursive italic) is emphasized in this self-instructional book. Paragraphs acquainting the student with a brief history of the origins of our letters, from cave paintings to copperplate, are used as the writing practice for both basic and cursive italic. Numerals, various adaptations of handwriting, timed writing, and a section on the use of the edged pen are also presented. Illustrated. 8 1/2" x 11" format. 5mm-4mm body height. 64 pp.

The **Instruction Manual** is to be used in conjunction with BOOKS A-G (kindergarten - 6th grade). Please note BOOK G is designed as a self-instruction workbook. The INSTRUCTION MANUAL describes basic italic and cursive italic lowercase joins 1-8, lifts and optional joins with emphasis on strokes, shape, size, slope, and spacing. Notes to teachers, teaching objectives, and assessment techniques are presented. Includes a rationale for italic handwriting, scope and sequence of the series, historical development of our alphabet and addresses special concerns such as left- or right-handedness. In addition, techniques for evaluation, increasing speed and developing a personal style, and complete information needed to effectively teach italic handwriting are discussed. The letter-size line guides and the examples of personal and business letters may be duplicated. 8½" x 11" format. 112 pp.

SUPPLEMENTARY MATERIALS

Basic Italic Alphabet Cards:
Attach to the wall to form a chart, or use individually as flash cards. Each card shows capital, lowercase letter and illustration; plus ten numerals cards. 36 card set, 4" x 6". For use with BOOKS A-C.

Cursive Italic Wall Chart:
Display as a reference for cursive italic capitals, lowercase and numerals. 10 card set, 18" x 6". For use with BOOKS D-G.

Basic and Cursive Italic Desk Strips:
Designed for the student as a ready reference to basic and cursive italic letter shapes.

- The basic italic desk strip contains lowercase, capitals and numerals. Set of 30 or individual strips, 16.5" x 3.5". For use with BOOKS A-C.

- The cursive italic desk strip has basic italic, cursive italic and cursive italic joins. Set of 30 or individual strips, 18" x 2.5" For use with BOOKS D-G.

- Laminated combined basic and cursive italic desk strip with numerals, 17" x 5.5". For use with BOOKS A-G.

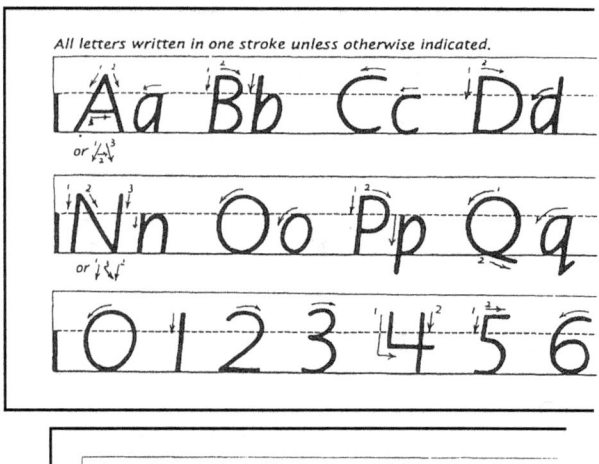

PARTIAL EXAMPLES OF DESK STRIPS — ONE-HALF SCALE

SEQUENCE OF WRITING SIZES WITHIN THIS SERIES

| 14mm | 11mm | 9mm | 6mm | 5mm | 4mm |
| Book A | Book B | Books B & C | Books C D E F | Books D E F G | Books F & G |

Components of the Getty-Dubay® Italic Handwriting Series

Blackline Masters: (Worksheets)
One CD providing supplementary writing practice pages to be used in conjunction with the *Getty-Dubay® Italic Handwriting Series*, BOOKS A-G. PDF format. Each printable sheet contains two lessons that reference the page number in the corresponding workbook. These Blackline half sheets may be reproduced copyright free for use as an introduction to the workbook page or as a review. Writing practice contains a single letter per half page for BOOKS A and B. Writing practice for BOOKS C-G contains single letters or short letter combinations. Frequent practice is important to consolidate learned hand movements.
Two half sheets on each 8 1/2" x 11" page.

Online Resources:
Visit www.handwritingsuccess.com for instructional videos, ruled lines, a Do-It-Yourself Worksheet Creator to make custom worksheets with your own text, and to purchase Getty-Dubay® products.

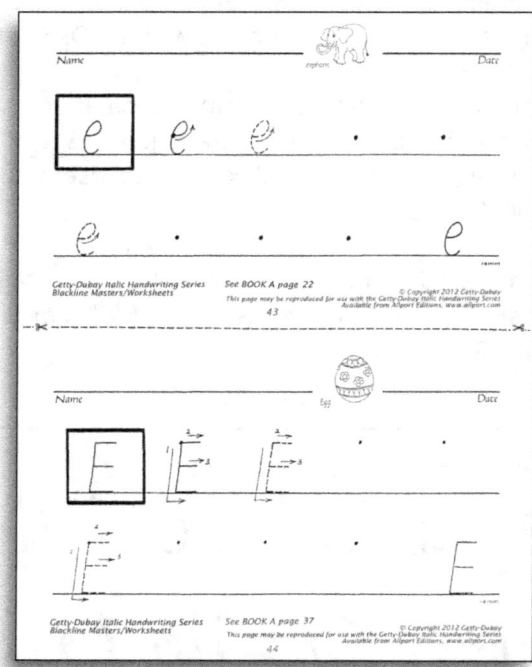
Sample page Blackline Master, BOOK A

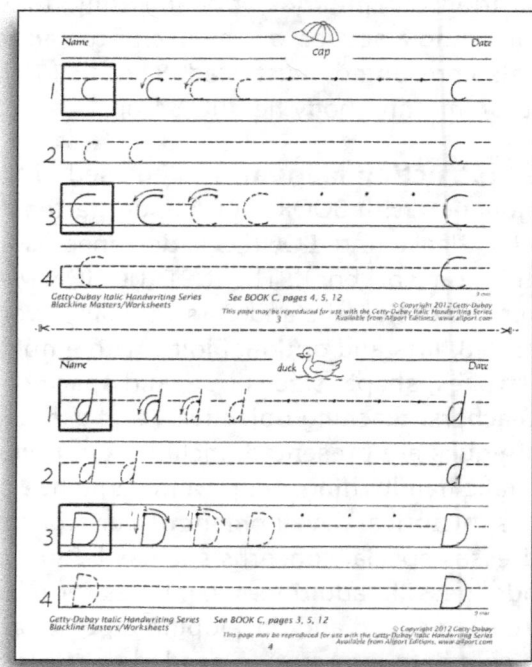
Sample page Blackline Master, BOOK C

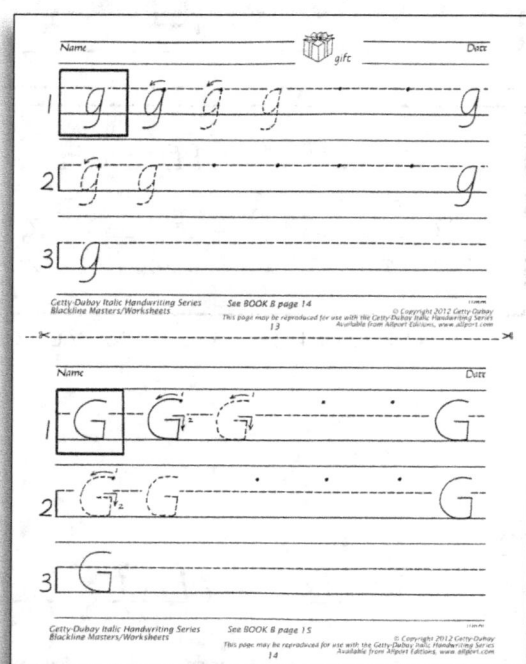
Sample page Blackline Master, BOOK B

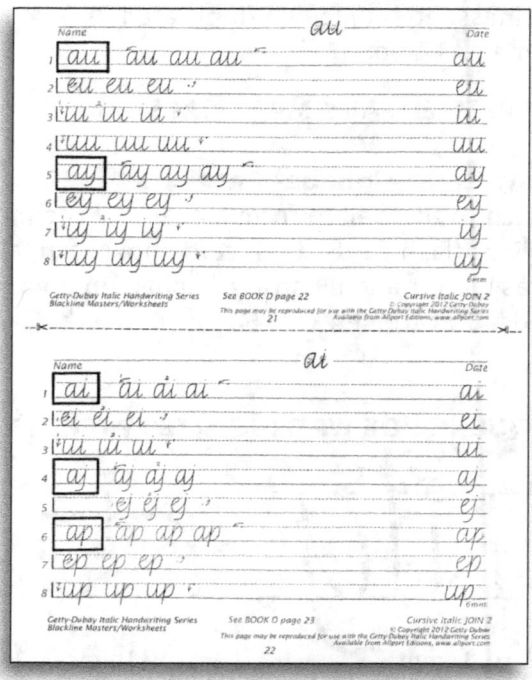
Sample page Blackline Master, BOOK D

Teaching Getty-Dubay® Italic Handwriting

Teaching Italic in the Elementary Classroom
The Beginning Writer
Special Concerns
Notes to Teachers
Letter Descriptions
Numerals
Cursive Join Descriptions
Sequence of Skills

· abcdefghijklmnopqrstuvwxyz ·

Teaching Italic in the Elementary Classroom

AN ELEMENTARY TEACHER'S PERSONAL VIEW

by Vicki Swartz

I am proud to say that my students' italic handwriting is *absolutely beautiful!* Their italic work on our classroom walls, in their topic books, and in the halls of the school has been noticed and commented on by visitors and staff. Many parents have thanked me for helping their child develop attractive, legible handwriting. "I never thought my child could write so beautifully," I've heard.

I especially felt pleased with the sustained growth in handwriting I saw with the students I stayed with for two or three years. In the final analysis, the better a teacher gets to know each child, the better job we can do teaching handwriting. I feel excited about the positive effects I see as nongraded multi-age grouping philosophies are increasingly implemented in our schools, where students learn to be accepting of the wide range of ability in the classroom community, and where students spend two or three years with their teacher.

Teachers have their own style of teaching handwriting and of working with their own unique students. There is no template, no "right" or "best" way to teach italic. I offer what has worked for me with seven to eleven year olds (second, third, fourth, and fifth graders) in the Portland Public Schools.

I teach two italic lessons a week and mark out about a 30-40 minute block of instructional time. I make overheads of the italic lines found in the back of the students' workbooks and write my own letters while the whole class faces the overhead screen. I teach the students the head, shoulder, foot, and ascender lines. I found making overheads of the workbook pages to be less effective. Teaching handwriting is one of the few subjects I teach to the whole group.

After modeling the letter or join, I purposely move to the next line and write correct and less correct models of letters to get feedback from the children. "Is there anything wrong with any of these joins?" I'll ask. I want them to be able to be careful observers, to visually discriminate and evaluate letter shapes and spacing. "Yes, that *w* is rounded and should be pointed, like two *v*'s," someone will say. "Yes, that join should be at the waistline, not the baseline," another will add, or "That one's too fat! And that *e* looks like it's leaning backwards, like it just slipped on a banana peel!" The students get so sharp at this visual evaluation that they start finding tiny faults with letters I had intended to be models of correctness.

> *"Many parents have thanked me for helping their child develop attractive, legible handwriting. 'I never thought my child could write so beautifully,' I've heard."*

Sometimes, I ask students to stand and trace the outline of the letter or join with a stiff arm as I talk it through. "Start at the shoulder line, go straight down and make a serif, lift your pencil arm and cross that *t* on the waistline . . ." I try to use *italic language* so we have this common understanding.

I have young children practice letter shapes with their finger in wet sand, or on a textured carpet sample. Sometimes I set up small groupings of kids to practice letters on lap chalkboards using chalk.

Vicki Swartz has 39 years of experience as an elementary educator. She has taught italic handwriting in the United States in Washington, Oregon, Georgia, Florida and in England as a Fulbright Exchange teacher. Her most recent position was Head of the Lower School at Catlin Gabel School, Portland, Oregon USA.

Vicki has taught early childhood development and a variety of curriculum courses to teachers at the university level, and has given workshops on teaching italic handwriting to youngsters. She is a 1999 inductee into the National Teachers Hall of Fame.

Teaching Italic Handwriting - by Vicki Swartz

I like how these mediums give valuable "practice" while forgiving rough initial efforts. It is certainly much easier to smooth out sand or erase a chalkboard than it is to erase letters firmly written in workbooks. We must accept children's initial "approximations" as this is how they learn to speak, read, and write our language. And of course, not every child has to do every page in the workbook.

So far what I have outlined does not seem particularly unusual or revolutionary. However, what I do during the students' actual practice time is what I feel makes the most difference. I move all over the classroom, leaning over students' shoulders and giving each student feedback at least two or three times during the next 20-30 minutes.

> *"It would take a keen observer to distinguish between feedback, evaluation, teaching, and learning, for they are not separate."*

My expectations are simple: I look for quality, not quantity, and my students know well that I would rather they practice a few lines on the workbook page *well* than rush through and finish the page. This takes a tremendous amount of pressure off my slower, struggling students who need to be given this permission. I do not compare, nor do I let my students compare how much they do with anyone but themselves.

My marking system is also straightforward. If a letter is a "Wow" letter, I place a star above it. If a letter needs fixing or redoing, I place a small dot above it. I do not usually say what is wrong with it ... I leave that up to the children to figure out through peer help. Once the letter has been fixed and meets my very high standards, I simply change the dot into a star and voila! You can't even see that there was once a dot there, providing a psychological gimmick to help students feel success and pride when they generally keep and work in the same italic handwriting workbook for several months at a time. (Would *you* like to be reminded permanently of your mistakes with permanent red marks or circles?!) If students finish early, they go on to other work after I have checked it. But most kids sustain their writing for the full practice session. If a student gets totally absorbed and wants more time, he/she is given more time.

The standard I hold for handwriting is very high. I have students redo work until it is their best even if this means redoing writing several times. This consistency is well worth it when students internalize this standard for themselves. "When she says it has to be in your best italic, it really does have to be in your best italic, or you'll have to do it all over again," I overheard a child in my classroom tell a new student. *The kids know!*

However, the standards I hold become individualized the better I get to know each student. Keeping the same students for three years I certainly knew their handwriting capabilities very, very well. I urged Michael who has impeccable writing to work on increasing his speed ... I asked Becky to mark dots over her own letters to show which needed correcting/improving ... I requested Sharika to choose two letters to focus upon on a page of nearly indecipherable attempts, knowing that she had eye-hand coordination problems. I had provided my own "dotted line" letter models for students who need an on-the-spot individualized lesson right on the side of their italic page. I simply masked the bottom half of the italic workbook page for Jason, with a severe learning disability, who became distressed at the threat of having to complete an entire page. You just do what you need to do with each child.

It would take a keen observer to distinguish between feedback, evaluation, teaching, and learning, for they are not separate.

I found the italic workbooks and the students' own topic work (final drafts of work done in their best writing mounted and sewn into a book) were like the living portfolios, for the children could readily examine their own handwriting for growth. When I asked them to carefully scrutinize their learning in italic and write about it, I was pleased with the results. "I used to get lots of dots, and now I don't," said one student. "My *a* used to be too round and now I know to make it have a flat top and a triangular shape, and it looks lots better," said another. Indeed, I could bring students to understand my emphasis on the letter family that includes *a, d, g,* and *q* as they examined their own work. They were thoroughly amazed to look at the sample of their best handwriting that I had them do the first week we were together. This paper, including the date and "This is my very best handwriting," the infamous "quick brown fox" sentence, and the alphabet, in both uppercase and lowercase, certainly received much mileage in the way of evaluation. It confirmed that the more we let children see the evidence of their own learning, the more empowered and capable they are of continuing such growth.

As we move into the establishment of nongraded classrooms that may have two or three age levels of students deliberately mixed together in a multi-age grouping, we teachers are being given permission to further individualize and personalize italic instruction. Not all students will need the same group lesson, but they will certainly still need instruction.

In multi-age classrooms I visited in Australia and England, I saw teachers trying different strategies of individualization. Some simply assigned students italic workbooks after an informal needs assessment (i.e., a third grader may really need the line size and spacing in the second grade book) and let the students march through the workbooks at their own pace. The children could pick up the workbooks and complete a page anytime during their classroom choice time. However, what resulted was a near elimination of teacher demonstrations and consistent feedback. (Who is going to go back, erase and redo five pages of poor work that slipped by unchecked?) The quality of handwriting suffered, I felt, with the general teacher nightmare of "I can't remember who is working on which letter when . . . " This, of course, can be kept track of but when teachers are already trying to collect data, observations, and assessments to personalize instruction in whole language in general, do we also need 28 students to be going 28 different ways in handwriting instruction?

The classes I observed that held a high value and standard on handwriting had frequent whole group or small group lessons that involved specific demonstrations followed up with practice. Each child would get and give feedback as peer tutors. The teacher monitored the quality of the work as well. "Handwriting is the only thing I still teach as a whole group lesson," commented one teacher of six to nine-year-olds.

The students were allowed to select the width of lines they would use for practice, and how many lines were done at a time. Lessons involved upward and downward extensions for students—practicing the basic *a* letter shape for the youngest class member, all the way to joining the *a* into other letters and words for the nine-year-old doing cursive on paper with skinnier lines. Pencils with triangular hand grips were available, if they chose to use them . . . edged ink pens, too. Students were empowered and trusted to make good choices in their italic learning. This level of trust expands as the teacher gets to know each student intimately over a two or three year period. Indeed, the line between italic handwriting lessons and daily writing begins to blur when standards and expectations are maintained throughout the school day.

> *"It confirmed that the more we let children see the evidence of their own learning, the more empowered and capable they are of continuing such growth."*

I am heartened that we teachers are finally being given permission to look at our curriculum differently—to look at how children's handwriting develops along a continuum of growth. We traditional teachers have much to benefit by also relaxing the rigid, lock-step, age-graded curricular expectations in order to better accommodate the very wide range of ability we have present in our regular classrooms, and taking some serious steps towards personalizing our instruction.

THE BEGINNING WRITER

The human hand can be considered one of the most precise instruments in existence and at times it becomes the means through which the intellect finds expression, as in handwriting. The perceptual judgments made and the accuracy with which the hands and fingers move are inseparable. Research indicates that there exists an almost perfect correlation between measures evaluating the children's *awareness* of their fingers and the ability to *use* their fingers in precise manual skills (Cratty, 14).

Readiness for handwriting is as important as readiness in reading (Barbe 1974), and there appear to be six prerequisite skill areas for handwriting:

1. small muscle development
2. eye-hand coordination
3. holding a writing tool
4. writing basic strokes
5. letter perception
6. orientation to printed language

When children first attempt to create letter forms, what they write may look like scribbling, but the scribbles will have certain characteristics of print. They may be arranged more horizontally than vertically and may be more linear than circular. These are the overall characteristics that children first use to judge whether or not their marks are writing. (Schickendanz, 73)

Activities to encourage readiness for handwriting:

- eye-hand coordination: activities such as buttoning, stringing beads, pasting, block building, finger painting, ball catching
- small muscle development: use of LEGOs, TINKERTOYs, snap beads, jigsaw puzzles, molding activities (clay, sand, cornmeal, dough), pounding nails, zipping, buttoning, screwing caps and/or nuts and bolts, tying knots and bows, painting, coloring, drawing, tracing, tearing, folding, cutting, following mazes on paper
- correct positioning of writing tool (standard pencil, ballpoint pen, fibertip pen, etc.)
- writing basic strokes

  \\\\\\\\   ⓞ ○ ○ ○ ○ ○   ┼ ┼ ┼ ┼ ┼ ┼
  ⼁𝓂𝓂𝓂𝓂   △ △ △ △ △ △   ⼁𝓊𝓊𝓊𝓊𝓊𝓊

- reading to children so they learn that print makes sense—that it is arranged in a meaningful way
- learning that speech and print are related

Typical indicators of readiness are when a student can:

- hammer nails
- build a tall tower of blocks
- copy simple LEGO models
- follow a maze on paper staying within the exterior lines
- color, copy, trace

Learning how to write involves much more than learning to write letters. It is a sophisticated and complex process including the following considerations. One step involves learning how to organize writing on the page which requires an understanding of spatial concepts. Another problem children have in putting their writing on paper has to do with spacing between words. Beginning writers often fail to leave space between words, but this does not necessarily indicate that they do not know that words exist as separate units (Temple et al, 41).

Children's own names are generally the first letters to be traced, copied, and eventually generated in their own handwriting—an exciting feat!

The teacher can lead children to find challenge and delight in the writing process by reading to them, modeling writing, providing writing materials, and especially by building enthusiasm for the written word.

Reminders from student workbooks
GETTY-DUBAY® ITALIC HANDWRITING SERIES
PROCESS, LETTER DIMENSIONS & ASSESSMENT

PROCESS
PENCIL HOLD
Use a soft lead pencil (#1 or #2) with an eraser. Hold the pencil with the thumb and index finger, resting on the middle finger. The upper part of the pencil rests near the large knuckle.

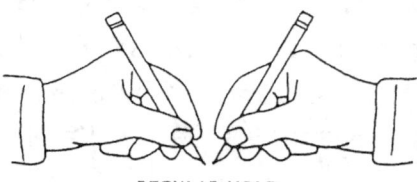
REGULAR HOLD

Hold the pencil firmly and lightly. AVOID pinching. To relax your hand, tap the index finger on the pencil three times.

Problem grips such as the 'thumb wrap' (thumb doesn't touch pencil) and the 'death grip' (very tight pencil hold) make it difficult to use the hand's small muscles. To relieve these problems, try this alternative pencil hold.

ALTERNATIVE HOLD

Place the pencil between the index finger and the middle finger. The pencil rests between the index and middle fingers by the large knuckles. Hold the pencil in the regular way at the tips of the fingers.

PAPER POSITION

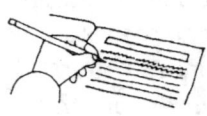

LEFT HANDED
If you are left-handed and write with the wrist below the line of writing, turn the paper clockwise so it is slanted to the right as illustrated. If you are left-handed and write with a "hook" with the wrist above the line of writing, turn the paper counter-clockwise so it is slanted to the left as illustrated (similar to the right-handed position).

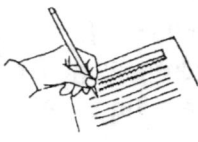

RIGHT-HANDED
If you are right-handed turn the paper counter-clockwise so it is slanted to the left as illustrated.

POSTURE
Rest your feet flat on the floor and keep your back comfortably straight without slumping. Rest your forearms on the desk. Hold the workbook or paper with your non-writing hand so that the writing area is centered in front of you.

STROKES

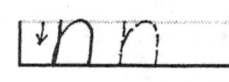

Basic italic letters all start at the top and go down or over (horizontal), except **d** and **e** (**d** starts at the waistline and **e** starts at the center of the body height).
Follow the direction of the arrow. Letters are written in one stroke unless otherwise indicated.

Trace the dotted line model, then copy model in space provided. If needed, trace solid line model.

PROCESS
For the teacher
Model correct pencil hold, paper position, and posture. If a student has a problem pencil hold, such as 'thumb wrap' or 'death grip', model the alternative pencil hold. Show the correct stroke direction and sequence of each letter and/or cursive join. Model on the chalkboard, on an overhead projector, on a writing slate, or on the student's paper. When modeling, use the vocabulary shown on the next page to describe the letter dimensions. It is helpful for the teacher and students to write the letters and joins in the air for large muscle kinesthetic learning. The students then write in the workbook and then on lined paper. Tracing the letters is helpful for small muscle kinesthetic learning.

See letter descriptions:
basic and cursive lowercase, pages 32–41
basic capitals, page 42
cursive capitals, page 43
numerals, page 44
cursive joins, page 45–49

LETTER DIMENSIONS

SHAPE
Basic italic lowercase letters are divided into eight families according to similarities in shape. Basic italic capitals are divided into three groups according to width. Cursive italic lowercase joins are divided into eight groups.
See *Shape Guidelines*, page 57.

SIZE
Letters are written with a consistent body height. Capitals, ascenders and descenders are written one and a half times the body height.
See *Size Guidelines*, page 58.

SLOPE
The models are written with a 5° letter slope. A consistent slope is an important part of good handwriting. For individual slope choices, see *Slope Guidelines*, page 59.

SPACING
Letters are written close together with even spacing within words. Joins are natural spacers in cursive italic; when lifts occur, keep letters close together.
Even spacing is used between words in a sentence.
See *Spacing Guidelines*, page 60.

SPEED
Write at a comfortable rate of speed that allows legible and neat handwriting. To increase the speed of writing, use the *Timed Writing, page 61*. See *Speed Guidelines*, page 60.

VOCABULARY

ASSESSMENT
Assessment is the key to improvement. The assessment method used enables the student and teacher to monitor progress. STEP 1: the student is asked to LOOK at the writing and affirm what is the best. Questions are asked requiring a yes/no answer. "Yes" is affirmation of a task accomplished. "No" indicates work to be done to improve writing. STEP 2: the student is asked to PLAN what needs to be improved and how to accomplish this. STEP 3: the student is asked to put the plan into PRACTICE. This *LOOK, PLAN, PRACTICE* format provides assessment skills applicable to all learning situations. Letter shape is the first focus in the program, followed by size, slope, spacing, and speed.

For the teacher: see *Assessment* pp. 54–55

For the student
GOAL
To write legible, neat handwriting.

- **LOOK** at your writing. Circle your best letter or join. Answer questions about strokes, shape, size, slope, or spacing.
- **PLAN** how to make your writing look more like the model. Pick the letter or join that needs work. Compare with the model.
- **PRACTICE** the letter or join that needs work. Write on the lines provided and on lined paper.
- Give yourself a star at the top of the page when you see you have made an improvement.

Note: BOOKS B and C have *LOOK* only.

SPECIAL CONCERNS

STUDENTS WITH DISABILITIES

In September, 1973, the United States 93rd Congress passed the Rehabilitation Act and in January, 1992, the Americans With Disabilities Act became law, amended by the ADA in 2008. Both laws stress equal opportunity, not merely equal treatment, to eliminate discrimination.

Students with learning disabilities

A "learning disability" affects the way a person with normal or above average intelligence takes in, retains, and/or expresses information. This information may become scrambled in one or more of the following areas: reading comprehension; written expression; spelling; math computation and problem-solving; organizational ability; time management; social interaction; spoken language; and/or visual, auditory, or tactile perception.

While some students may have had their learning disabilities identified, many will have not. It is important that the instructor provides an especially supportive environment for those with diagnosed learning disabilities and those the instructor suspects may have learning problems. Over the years, teachers and parents may have mistakenly attributed students' learning problems to low motivation or intellectual disabilities. Seek special testing if available.

Students with learning disabilities will have greater success at learning if all sense modalities can be used in the teaching-learning process: visual, auditory, tactile and kinesthetic. (Palmer, Robert, et al.)

For students with learning disabilities, a handwriting model must be consistent, unambiguous, and resistant to deterioration. This allows speed and legibility to be not only gained, but maintained, throughout childhood, the teen years, and adulthood. (Gladstone, 1995) In Getty-Dubay® Handwriting, the structure of every letter remains consistent throughout the program. A letter that starts at the top always starts at the top — a letter beginning with a downstroke always begins with a downstroke. Even when it joins other letters, the letter *m* should look like *m*, the letter *n* like *n,* etc. Clear, consistent shapes, designed to fit natural movements of our hands, encourage speed even when letters do not join. Writing without joins in Getty-Dubay® basic italic allows one to build speed and legibility, making basic italic an extremely practical choice for those who have learning disabilities or who just prefer the simplest possible option for practical handwriting. (Gladstone, 1995)

Students on the autism spectrum

Handwriting issues are prevalent among students who have Asperger's syndrome or other autism spectrum conditions. (Kushki et al., 2011). According to Kate Gladstone, a handwriting instructor who herself is on the autism spectrum, the handwriting difficulties of students with autism involve both motor issues and perceptual issues. Both types of issues are greatly reduced when handwriting models avoid unnecessary elements, e.g., loops, and allow for the omission of the less practical joins. Effects of perceptual issues are further reduced and may be eliminated when the structure of each letter remains constant throughout the entire handwriting program and when it can be logically related to the structure of other letter forms that the student will encounter. This is why the Getty-Dubay® program's instruction on relationships among different letter styles — basic italic, cursive italic and looped cursive, the latter pp. 50 & 51 — is especially helpful for students on the autism spectrum. (Gladstone, 2013)

Students with mobility impairments and other physical challenges

"Mobility impairment" is a term that refers to a wide range of disabilities including orthopedic, neuromuscular, cardiovascular, and pulmonary disorders. Other impairments include mental health disorders, visual and auditory impairments and intellectual disabilities. All will require special accommodations. (Palmer, Robert, et al.)

Special Concerns
OF SPECIAL INTEREST
Italic handwriting has an advantage over other handwriting programs as the letterforms for basic italic (printing) and cursive italic are the same, allowing the student to build on previously learned concepts. Even though the task in cursive italic is to join most letters, there are some students who prefer to leave letters unjoined. *Students who have trouble remembering motor sequences and/or visualizing letters may prefer printing rather than cursive writing. Please invite them to use Basic Italic for their everyday handwriting!*

LEFT- AND RIGHT-HANDED WRITERS
The right-handed person has a natural tendency to begin at the left-hand margin and write toward the right. The writing instrument is moved from left to right and the writer can view what has just been written. However, the left-handed person must contend with the added difficulty of pushing the writing tool from left to right. As the left-handed person writes a line, the words are often obscured. Some left-handers compensate by adopting a style of writing known as the "hook," where the hand is held above the writing line.

RIGHT-HANDED PAPER POSITION (slanted counter-clockwise)

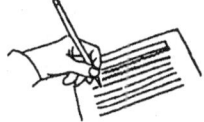
LEFT-HANDED PAPER POSITION WRIST ABOVE WRITING LINE ("hook" position)

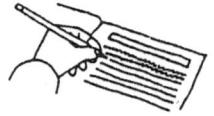
LEFT-HANDED PAPER POSITION WRIST BELOW WRITING LINE (slanted clockwise)

Left-handed writers need special consideration, especially in the early years when they are forming handwriting strategies. All school work can be affected if care is not taken to ensure the success of the left-handed writer. The following common sense rules are well documented: (Sassoon)

1. Workbook or paper should be placed to the writer's left side, then slanted to suit the student. This permits writers to have their hand below the line allowing full vision of their letters as they write.

2. Appropriate lighting is necessary to make sure left-handers are not writing in the shadow of their own hand. A seat height that allows writers to see over their writing hand is essential. See *Posture*, p. 14.

3. Non-smudging pencils available in art supply stores and permanent pens are widely available. Both are recommended for left-handed writers.

4. **The writing instrument needs to be held far enough from the point to allow the writer to see what has just been written. The index finger can be as near to the point as the writer wishes, but the thumb may need to be held back a bit.**

All beginning writers must be taught that we read and write beginning at the left, but left-handers may need much more practice in left-to-right

Some left-handers write with a "hook," as shown in the illustration. The authors believe that this often occurs because young children are reminded to slant their paper to the left, when indeed the left-handers should slant their paper to the right. In any event, do not attempt to change the student's paper slant or to change the student's writing hand from left to right. You can assist both left- and right-handed students by emphasizing a comfortable pencil and paper hold.

We encourage you, as the instructor, to do some practice writing with your non-writing hand so that you are able to understand what difficulties are presented to writers of either hand. Your letterforms will not be spectacular, but you will gain an understanding of your students' needs, and all of you will probably have a good laugh about your writing!

Do not attempt to change the student's writing hand from left to right.

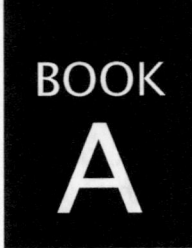

GETTY-DUBAY® ITALIC HANDWRITING SERIES – NOTES TO TEACHERS

ASSESSMENT:

Until now our educational system has been oriented to the standardized test. But currently, educators are realizing that teachers, children, and caregivers must share in decisions and control about learning; that assessment and instruction are ongoing processes that are interdependent; and that content and skills are learned in integrated purposeful settings (Glazer, 8).

The Getty-Dubay® Italic Handwriting Series provides a self-assessment process, LOOK, PLAN, PRACTICE, to enable the student to monitor progress. LOOK, step one of this process, begins in this book, BOOK A.

This book is for beginning writers. To enable young students to consider their own progress, self-assessment references are made on some student pages beginning on p. 2. Please assist early readers with the self-assessment process.

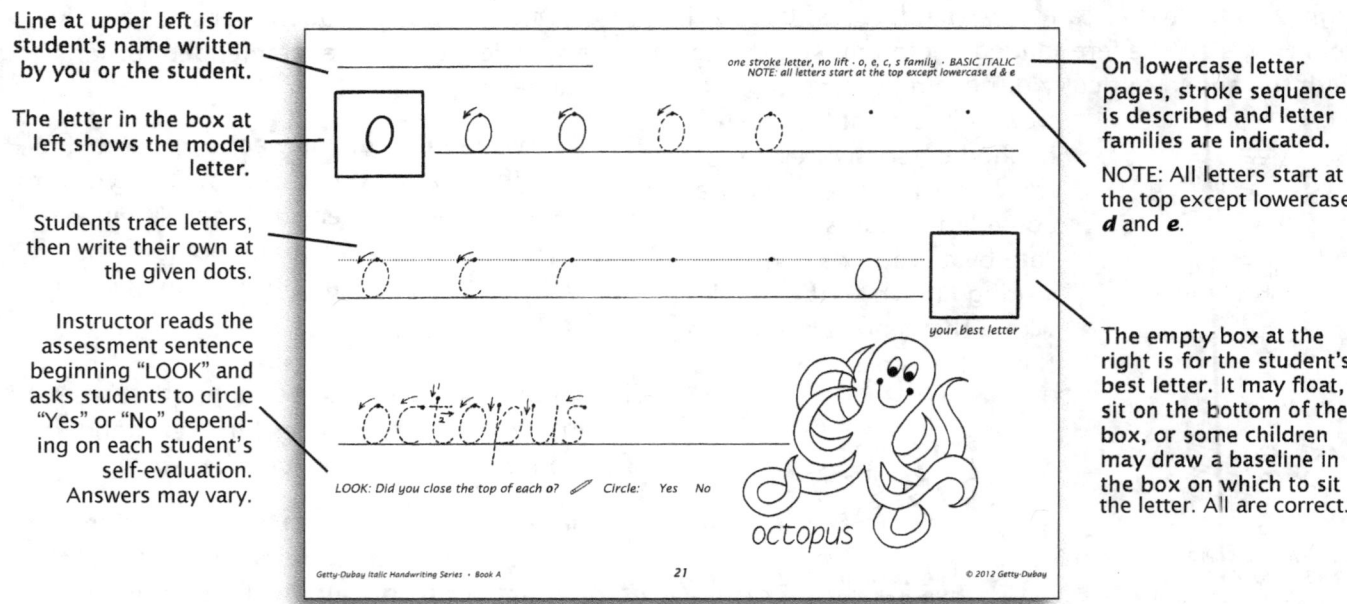

PAGES IN BOOK A

We read lowercase letters 98% of the time (Catich 1977), therefore we have arranged BOOK A so that lowercase letters are presented on the first side of the book, one letter per page, beginning with Family 1. The corresponding capital form is on the reverse page.

This is the proper time to introduce comfortable pencil hold. We recommend standard size pencils for your students rather than the thicker ones. Refer to p. 14 in this book and the *Introduction* (p. iii) and *Reminders* (p. vi) in BOOK A.

Workbook page reference:

vii Have students practice these movements one at a time with crayons, felt markers, paint brushes, and/or pencils on plain paper before doing a particular line or lines in the book. Also have students "write" these practice movements in the air, in cornmeal, etc. Call the line the *baseline* and ask students to "bump" the line, or touch it when writing in the book. Do use a consistent vocabulary! Refer to p. 15 in this MANUAL and *Reminders* in BOOK A.

4 Watch that the student makes **k** with ascender) not **K** for the lowercase form.

9 Call the curve of **h** the *arch*. Demonstrate on the board how the curved lined branches away from the *downstroke* to make the arch, but don't worry about teaching the vocabulary. Do it as you teach, and your students will learn from you as you use the words over and over.

17 Here is the *basic a* shape once again, but this time it ends below the waistline. You might say, "The letter **g** lives in the basement," or use whatever terminology you generally use when teaching letters with descenders. Young children like to call it a *descender*, too, because that's the 'grown-up' way.

19 Note that lowercase **b** ends with a horizontal line on the baseline. Demonstrate a large letter on the chalkboard, butcher paper, in the air or overhead projector. Say, "Move along the baseline to close **b**."

21 Help students avoid making a point at the top of **o** by demonstrating how to overlap the beginning of the letter.

Getty-Dubay® Italic Handwriting Series - Notes to Teachers: BOOK A

CLASSROOM MANAGEMENT:
It is important that handwriting be presented with direct instruction, especially for the young writer. It is up to you to decide the manner in which you present letters and/or words in relationship with your reading program. Do model the letters and words daily after you begin your BOOK A handwriting program. Spend 5 to 10 minutes a day at first in direct handwriting instruction, increasing the time as your students build an interest in handwriting. Find ways to integrate letters and words they have learned to write into other areas of your curriculum.

From day one, have BASIC ITALIC DESK STRIPS and ALPHABET CARDS available for student use. For extra practice, use BLACKLINE MASTERS. (See pp. 7 & 8.)

As your program progresses, each week have students save at least one page of handwriting of their choice to be included in their individual portfolios.

NOTE: Teachers who run highly individualized programs in the classroom setting report handwriting is one subject that is easily presented to the entire group.

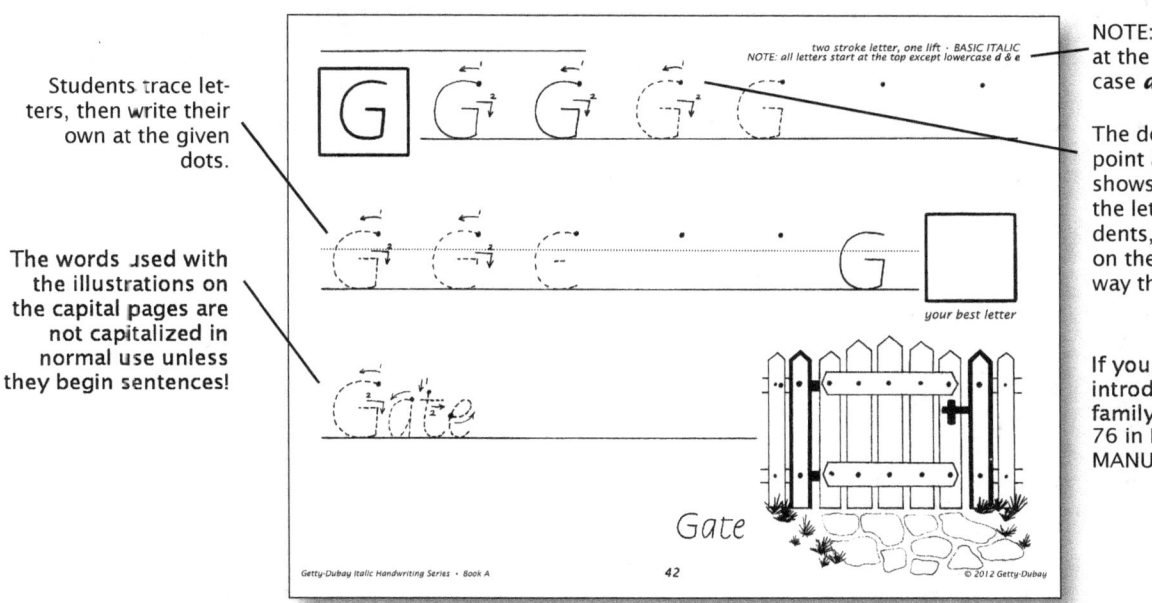

Students trace letters, then write their own at the given dots.

The words used with the illustrations on the capital pages are not capitalized in normal use unless they begin sentences!

NOTE: All letters start at the top except lowercase *d* and *e*.

The dot is a beginning point and the arrow shows the way to trace the letter. Tell your students, "Put your pencil on the dot and go the way the arrow points."

If you prefer to introduce capitals by family groups, see p. 76 in INSTRUCTION MANUAL.

26 If students have difficulty writing *t* with the ending curve, have them use a straight *t*.

31 Demonstrate the *basic a* shape above the baseline then make a downstroke to complete *q*.

37 Demonstrate capital *E* by making an *L* shape as the first stroke.

42 Say, "Make a *C* first. Then put your pencil in the middle of the *C*, make a line over and down to make *G*."

59 - 65 Review of lowercase families

To help young children understand that all letters (except *d* and *e*) start at the top and go down or over, have them repeat as a fun 'song,' "All letters start at the top and go down or over." Have your students decide how to say or sing it—loudly, softly, quickly, slowly, etc.

See INSTRUCTION MANUAL

LETTER DESCRIPTIONS
Basic italic lowercase, pages 32-41
Basic italic capitals, page 42

LETTER DIMENSIONS
Options, page 56
Shape Guidelines, page 57
Size Guidelines, page 58
Slope Guidelines, page 59
Spacing Guidelines, page 60

ASSESSMENT QUESTIONS
Basic italic lowercase, pages 62-63
Basic italic capitals, page 64

SELF-ASSESSMENT FOR THE YOUNG WRITER
1. Ask the student to LOOK at a line of his/her own writing and choose his/her best letter.
2. Ask the student to circle his/her best letter with a pencil or crayon.
3. Teacher supplies student with some feedback and reinforcement.

A PLAN FOR EFFICIENT USE OF DIRECT INSTRUCTION TIME

1. Students have sharpened pencils available.

2. Students have workbooks available in desks or teacher and students have a system for quick distribution.

3. Teacher provides overview of the day's lesson, introducing a letter or word *before* students open to the correct page in the workbook.

4. After discussion and practice of the letter or word, *then* workbooks are opened and students write the lesson.

5. Teacher circulates classroom helping students individually.

6. Student and teacher assess the day's work.

BOOK B

GETTY-DUBAY® ITALIC HANDWRITING SERIES – NOTES TO TEACHERS

ASSESSMENT

Until now our educational system has been oriented to the standardized test. But currently, educators are realizing that teachers, students, and caregivers must share in decisions and control about learning; that assessment and instruction are ongoing processes that are interdependent; and that content and skills are learned in integrated purposeful settings (Glazer, 8).

The *Getty-Dubay® Italic Handwriting Series* provides a self-assessment process, LOOK, PLAN, PRACTICE, to enable the student to monitor progress. LOOK, step one of this process, begins in BOOK A.

CLASSROOM MANAGEMENT

It is important that handwriting be presented with direct instruction, especially for the young writer. It is up to you to decide the manner in which you present letters and/or words in relationship with your reading program. Do model the letters and words.

The letter in the box shows the model letter.

Students trace letters, then write their own at the given dots. Each letter page may be divided into two lessons. See *Pages in BOOK B*, 2 below.

It is important for the students to understand the dot is a beginning point, not part of the letter, and that the arrow shows the way to go. Say, "Put your pencil on the dot and go the way the arrow points."

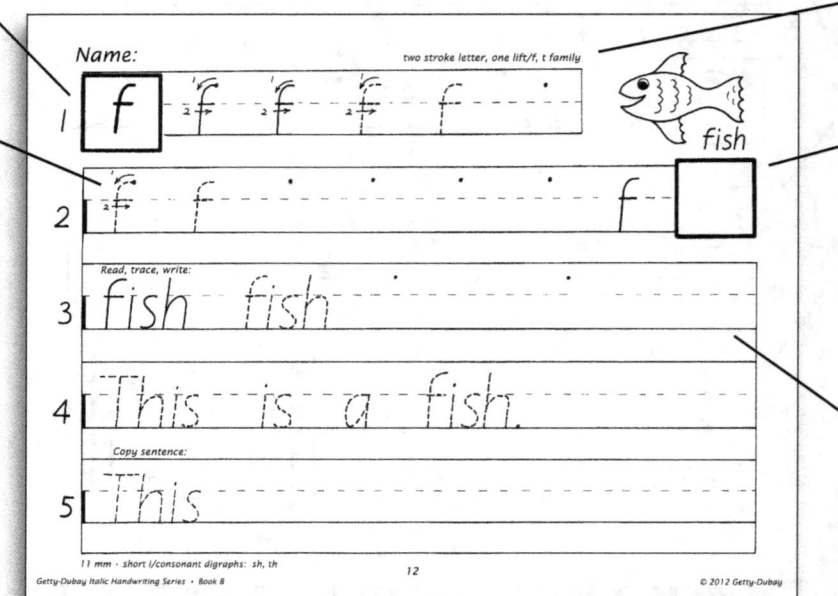

On lowercase letter pages, stroke sequence is described and letter familes are listed.

The empty box is for the student's best letter. The letter may float, sit on the bottom of the box, or some children may draw a baseline in the box on which to sit the letter. All are correct.

There are 5 lines for writing on pages 1-28, with a space of 11 mm from baseline to waistline, *body height*, the height of lowercase letters without ascenders or descenders.

PAGES IN BOOK B:

BOOK B is arranged one letter per page in alphabetical order, lowercase first and then capitals. Introduce letters according to the way in which you teach reading or introduce them by family groups.

Have students date each page in the workbook and pages from other written work, then have them file at least two or three papers into their own portfolios each week. (Young children easily learn to file their own papers—allow them to be responsible for their own work.)

1 Help students understand dot is the beginning point and not part of the letter, and that the arrow shows the way to go. Say, "Put your pencil on the dot and go the way the arrow points." Have students practice each of these exercises on plain paper with a variety of writing instruments, crayons, felt markers, pens, pencils, before completing the workbook page. Have students complete one or two lines at a time—the entire page all at once may be confusing.

2 Since many young students may not be reading when beginning this workbook, you may choose to have them complete the first two lines of each page. As they become more proficient reading words and sentences, they finish the page. Words are spaced far apart to assist the beginning reader. Have students begin the ***a, d, g, q*** family letters with a "flat head," a short horizontal line from right to left. See p.15 in this MANUAL and *Reminders* in BOOK B.

3 Capitals begin halfway between the waistline and ascender line. Teach the term "halfway" and call it "capital height." Demonstrate that the **A** horizontal line, stroke 3, is written below the waistline.

4 When introducing ***b***, discuss the branching line. Draw a branching line, an 'imaginary' line between the baseline and waistline. Demonstrate writing the downstroke, following

branching line →

back up to the branching line, curving up to the waistline, curving down to the baseline, and completing ***b*** by moving left on the baseline.

10 The ***e*** begins at the 'imaginary' branching line. (See notes for page 4.) Teach students to begin the letter halfway between the baseline and waistline— which is the branching line.

20 Pronounce *Julio* as you would in English, not in Spanish.

27 We have found the stroke sequence for ***M*** as shown works best for the beginning writer, but use a 4-stroke left-to-right sequence if you prefer.

33 *Putu*, m, Eskimo.

32 This is the first 'pencil picture' in BOOK B. It indicates the student is to circle *Yes* or *No*. Of course, this answer is an arbitrary one—the student's choice. This is also the first

daily after you begin your BOOK B handwriting program. Spend 5 to 10 minutes a day at first, increasing direct handwriting instruction time to a period of 15 to 20 minutes four or five times a week. This instruction together with opportunities for integrating handwriting into other areas of the curriculum can provide 25 to 30 minutes of practice four or five times a week.

From day one, have BASIC ITALIC DESK STRIPS and ALPHABET CARDS available for student use. For extra practice, use BLACKLINE MASTERS. (See pp. 7 & 8.)

As your program progresses, each week have students save at least one page of handwriting of their choice to be included in their individual portfolios.

NOTE: Teachers who run highly individualized programs in the classroom setting report handwriting is one subject that is easily presented to the entire group.

The writing lines are numbered for easy reference when talking with students.

Introduce vocabulary on the page before you have students "Read, trace, write."

The vertical black line between the baseline and the waistline indicates the body height of the letter, the space in which the letter fits without considering the ascender and/or descender.

There are 6 lines for writing on pages 29 to 56, with a space of 9 mm body height from baseline to waistline.

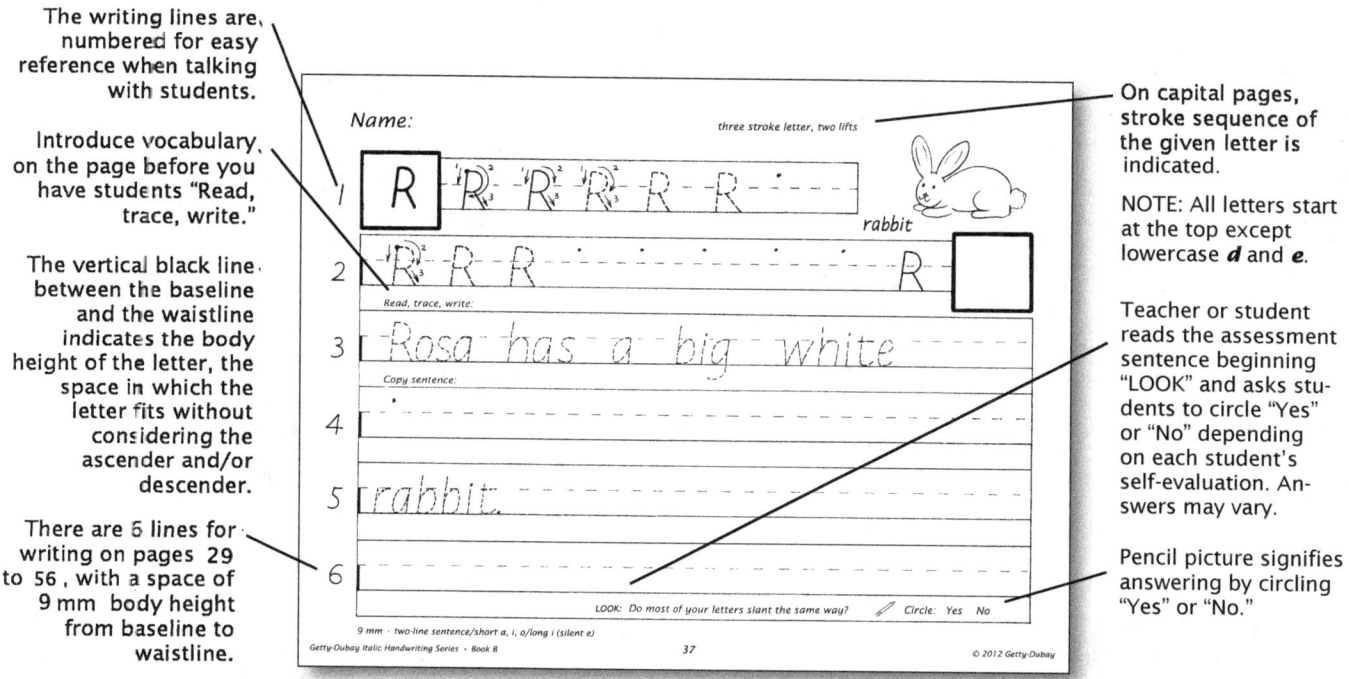

On capital pages, stroke sequence of the given letter is indicated.

NOTE: All letters start at the top except lowercase *d* and *e*.

Teacher or student reads the assessment sentence beginning "LOOK" and asks students to circle "Yes" or "No" depending on each student's self-evaluation. Answers may vary.

Pencil picture signifies answering by circling "Yes" or "No."

page with a two-line sentence, so do assist your students. We suggest writing the sentence with them on the chalkboard or whiteboard.

35 ✏ This is the first page with a student self-assessment question. Please talk with your students about looking at their **Q**, then have them circle their answer.

40 *Tunu*, f. Eskimo. This is the first page with 3 "pencil pictures", so give your students some extra help.

48 This is the first page where the student has a two-line sentence in sequence. We suggest that, on the overhead or chalkboard, you demonstrate sentences written in a similar manner. Have the students write along with you before they complete the workbook page.

Writing on a chalkboard or whiteboard is a terrific way to teach handwriting. Let the students take turns writing letters and/or words on the board. It's helpful to keep a student list and check off a name as each has an opportunity to individually write at the board.

Beginning writers quite often fail to leave spaces between words; however, this should not be taken to indicate that they don't know that words exist as separate units. Leaving spaces is a highly abstract procedure for children to manage. (Temple, 41)

See INSTRUCTION MANUAL

LETTER DESCRIPTIONS
Basic italic lowercase, pages 32-41
Basic italic capitals, page 42

LETTER DIMENSIONS
Options, page 56
Shape Guidelines, page 57
Size Guidelines, page 58
Slope Guidelines, page 59
Spacing Guidelines, page 60

ASSESSMENT QUESTIONS
Basic italic lowercase, pages 62-63
Basic italic capitals, page 64

A PLAN FOR EFFICIENT USE OF DIRECT INSTRUCTION TIME

1. Students have sharpened pencils available.

2. Students have workbooks available in desks or teacher and students have a system for quick distribution.

3. Teacher provides overview of the day's lesson, introducing a letter, word and/or sentence *before* students open to the correct page in the workbook.

4. After discussion and practice of the letter, word and/or sentence, *then* workbooks are opened and students write the lesson.

5. Teacher circulates classroom helping students individually.

6. Student and teacher assess the day's work.

GETTY-DUBAY® ITALIC HANDWRITING SERIES – NOTES TO TEACHERS

ASSESSMENT
Until now our educational system has been oriented to the standardized test. But currently, educators are realizing that teachers, students, and caregivers must share in decisions and control about learning; that assessment and instruction are ongoing processes that are interdependent; and that content and skills are learned in integrated purposeful settings. (Glazer, 8).

The *Getty-Dubay® Italic Handwriting Series* provides a self-assessment process, LOOK, PLAN, PRACTICE, to enable the student to monitor progress. LOOK, step one of this process, begins in BOOK A.

CLASSROOM MANAGEMENT It is important that handwriting be presented with direct instruction, especially for the young writer. It is up to you to decide the manner in which you present letters and/or words in relationship with your reading program.

NOTE: All letters start at the top except lowercase *d* and *e*.

The letter in the box shows the model letter.

Remind students to trace the models before writing their own letters and words.

It is important that the students understand the dot is a beginning point, not part of the letter, and that the arrow shows the way to go. Say, "Put your pencil on the dot and write the way the arrow points."

LOOK indicates student is to look at his/her writing and answer a specific question.

Student writes "best" letter in the empty box. The letter may float, sit on the bottom of the box, or some children may draw a baseline in the box on which to sit the letter. All are correct.

Pages 1-28 have spaces of 9mm from baseline to waistline, *body height*, the height of lowercase letters without ascenders or descenders.

Pencil picture means "circle" or answer "Yes" or "No."

Research indicates that at both the elementary and secondary levels, papers with neater, more legible handwriting generally receive higher scores than those with poor handwriting, *regardless* of the quality of content (Markham, 1976). It is essential that students develop a legible style of handwriting for their own personal use—instruction in handwriting should not be left to chance.

From time to time, with your students review: a comfortable, non-pinching pencil hold and a comfortable sitting position. While sitting at one of their own desks, demonstrate these points and also show them that their non-writing hand can move the paper as writing is accomplished so that the writing area remains in front of the writer.

Help students learn to use simple headings for papers and to leave adequate margins when using lined paper.

NOTES FOR BOOK C:

1 Introduce or review vocabulary words one or two at a session: ascender, descender, body height, baseline, waistline, etc., as shown in the illustration on page 1, BOOK C. Review letters one family at a time.

5 At the beginning of the year, you may have students fill in lines 1, 3, 5 & 7, then later fill in the words. Remind students to put their "best" letter in each empty box. Help students complete the self-assessment at the bottom of the page after they have finished the entire page.

8 You will need an unabridged dictionary to find the word *norimon*.

12 Aataq, m., Eskimo

16 Quyen, m., Asian.

21 Line 11 is only to be traced. Have students write it out on notebook paper.
   Students trace lines 12 and 13 then copy them on lines 14 and 15.

29 From here on the models are written with solid lines, but students need to continue tracing models before writing their own.

34 & 35 We recommend that students complete 4 lines per handwriting session.

39 Have students practice writing entrance and exit serifs on notebook paper.

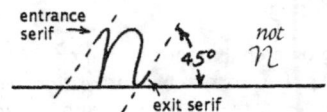

Getty-Dubay® Italic Handwriting Series - Notes to Teachers: BOOK C

Do model the letters and words daily after you begin your BOOK C handwriting program. Spend 15 to 20 minutes four or five times a week in direct handwriting instruction. This instruction, together with opportunities for integrating handwriting into other areas of the curriculum can provide 25 to 40 minutes of practice four or five times a week.

From day one, have BASIC ITALIC DESK STRIPS and ALPHABET CARDS available for student use. For extra practice, use BLACKLINE MASTERS. (See pp. 7 & 8.)

As your program progresses, each week have students save at least one page of handwriting of their choice to be included in their individual portfolios.

NOTE: Teachers who run highly individualized programs in the classroom setting report handwriting is one subject that is easily presented to the entire group.

Callouts on workbook page sample:
- Remind students to trace the models, both large and small, before writing their own joins and sentences.
- Letter joins that have already been introduced are underlined.
- Writing on first line of each join is larger for ease in establishing correct handwriting movements.
- Student writes "best" join in the empty box. The letters may float, sit on the bottom of the box, or some children may draw a baseline in the box on which to sit the joined letters. All are correct.
- Pages 29-37 and 42-58 have spaces of 6 mm from baseline to waistline.
- As joins are introduced on pages 42-52, each lesson includes a join description.
- That's celery!

42-52 Joins are used for speed and convenience only and generally are not used when writing large, as in introductory models shown on pp. 42-52. However, this large size helps students see and feel the joining of letters together for cursive italic.

42-52 Introduce the joins one lesson at a time. All joins are underlined. After tracing and copying in the workbook, have students practice joining letters and words on notebook paper.

44 Introduce one join at a time. All joins are underlined.

47 Say, "branch into *u* ," as in *au, du, lu, nu*, etc.

54 Write student's name in your best cursive italic, then student traces your writing and copies it on blank space below.

See INSTRUCTION MANUAL

LETTER DESCRIPTIONS
Basic and cursive italic lowercase, pp 32-41
Basic italic capitals, page 42
Transition and cursive italic joins, pp 45-49

LETTER DIMENSIONS
Options, page 56
Shape Guidelines, page 57
Size Guidelines, page 58
Slope Guidelines, page 59
Spacing Guidelines, page 60

ASSESSMENT QUESTIONS
Basic italic lowercase, pp 62-63
Basic italic capitals, page 64
Cursive italic lowercase joins, page 66

A PLAN FOR EFFICIENT USE OF DIRECT INSTRUCTION TIME

1. Students have sharpened pencils available.
2. Students have workbooks available in desks or teacher and students have a system for quick distribution.
3. Teacher provides overview of the day's lesson, introducing a letter, word, cursive join and/or sentence *before* students open workbook to the correct page. (Joins begin on p. 42.)
4. After discussion and practice of the letter, word, cursive join and/or sentence, *then* workbooks are opened and students write the lesson.
5. Teacher circulates classroom helping students individually.
6. Student and teacher assess the day's work.

BOOK D

GETTY-DUBAY® ITALIC HANDWRITING SERIES – NOTES TO TEACHERS

ASSESSMENT

STEP 1: Direct the student to LOOK at his/her writing and affirm what is the best. Questions are asked requiring a yes/no answer. 'Yes' is affirmation of a task accomplished. 'No' indicates work to be done to improve writing.

STEP 2: Direct the student to PLAN what needs to be improved and how to accomplish this.

STEP 3: Direct the student to put the plan into PRACTICE.

Direct the student to look over a week's writing practice and find a page showing the most improvement. The student then stars the page at the top and tells (teacher or student) how the writing has improved.

Provide the opportunity for each student to select a page of his/her best handwriting to include in the student's portfolio.

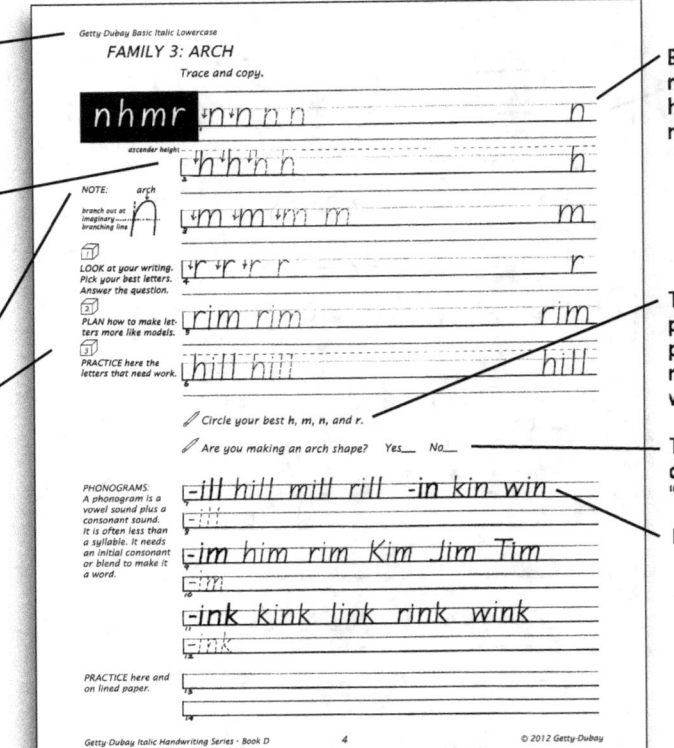

Margins contain information, directions, notes, hints, reminders, options, and assessment LOOK, PLAN, PRACTICE.

Trace and copy. Trace dotted model, then copy on lines provided and on lined paper. If needed, also trace solid line model.

NOTE for special attention.

Basic italic models are on the right-hand side for the left-hander who often covers up the models when he/she writes.

The student circles his/her personal best. It may not be perfect, but it is the best at the moment. Assessment begins with success and affirmation.

The student answers the question by checking "Yes" or "No."

Phonogram.

ASSESSMENT

1. LOOK at the writing. Direct the student to circle his/her personal best letter or join. Compare with the models.

2. PLAN: Assist the student in choosing letters that need work to improve the writing. Look at the letter dimensions of shape, size, slope, and spacing. Focus on one at a time. Begin with shape, then size, slope, and spacing. To assess, identify (1) what is going well, (2) what needs to be improved, and (3) what needs to be done to make the improvement. See *IM Assessment*, pages 54-55.

3. PRACTICE writing, making the improvements.

PAGES IN BOOK D:

vi-vii *Go over Reminders*, especially Process: pencil position, paper position, stroke direction and sequence.

2 Pencil picture means "circle" or answer "Yes" or "No."

2-11 Review basic italic or introduce italic to those new to the program. Ascender and capital height is halfway between waistline and line above. Lines used for basic italic writing are similar to lines in BOOK C.

4-9 Phonograms.

12-15 A few rules of capitalization are shown, including rules for spacing and slope lines. Assist students with lines they need to complete.

16 Emphasize continuing use of basic italic—lifelong! Encourage students to find improvements they have made and reward themselves with a star or two at the top of the page.

18-19 Build on previously learned concepts for cursive italic.

20-45 The eight cursive lowercase joins are presented sequentially. The words use only the joins that have been introduced. The body height is 6mm.

21 Optional join into *n*, *m*, *r*, and *x* using Join 2 (Also see page 27).

23 Option to use jot or dot. Left-handers may be more comfortable writing the jot from upper right to lower left.

26 Optional join into *n*, *m*, *r*, and *x* is offered. Some students do this join naturally. If it happens, encourage its use. The only difference is the soft angle entrance serif is left off and the join blends into the letter at the branching line.

32-33 BOOK D shows a lift between *t* and *e*; also a lift between *f* and *e*. Optional joins from *t* and *f* into *e* are shown on page 48 of the INSTRUCTION MANUAL and are presented in BOOKS E, F, & C.

31, 34, 35 Options for joins out of *o*, *v*, *w*, and *x* show modified joins and lifts.

33 Encourage students to follow the slope used in the workbook. At the same time, it is important to be aware that each student has his/her own natural slope. Use the assessment exercise in *Slope Guidelines*, page 77, to help the student find his/her most comfortable slope. Use

Getty-Dubay® Italic Handwriting Series - Notes to Teachers: BOOK D

CLASSROOM MANAGEMENT
Using direct instruction, present two pages a week, with follow-up practice on lined paper. Allow 20 minutes per page. Demonstrate the *Process, Letter Dimensions,* and *Assessment* for letters and joins. (See pages 14-15.)

Opportunities can be found for further handwriting practice by integrating italic handwriting into other areas of curriculum for 10-15 minutes daily.

PLAN FOR EFFICIENT USE OF DIRECT INSTRUCTION TIME:
1. Students have sharpened pencils on hand.
2. Students have workbooks on hand or a system provided for quick distribution of workbooks (books remain closed until after teacher models letters).
3. Teacher has pre-lined chalkboard or lined transparencies for overhead projector.
4. Teacher writes the page number on chalkboard and models letters.
5. Students write in workbooks.
6. Students and teacher assess writing.

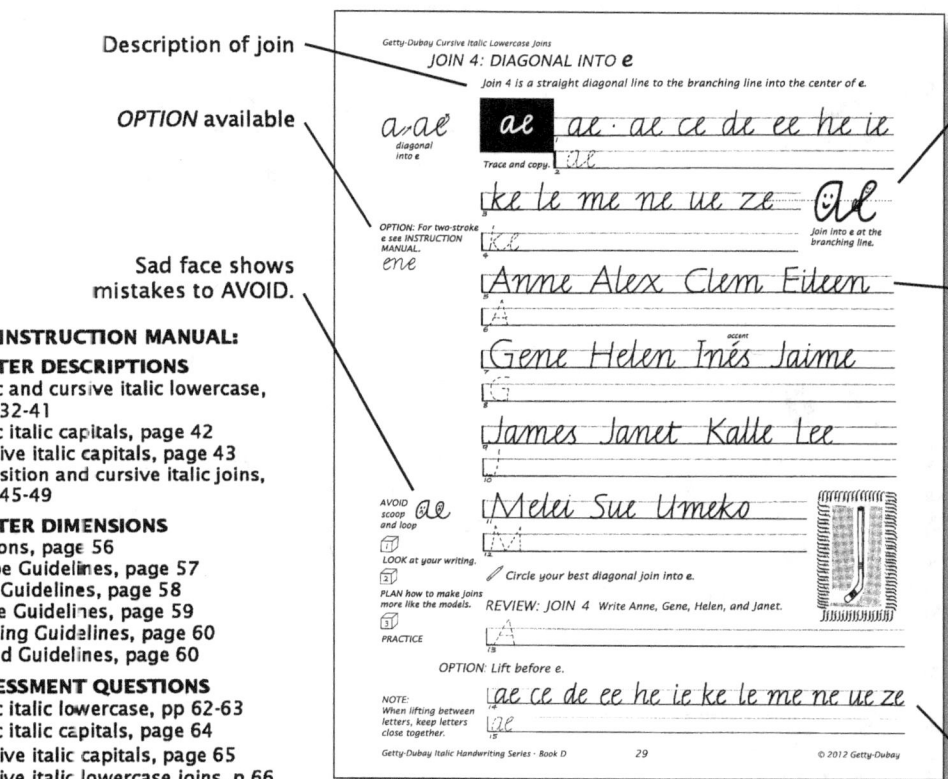

Description of join
OPTION available
Sad face shows mistakes to AVOID.

See INSTRUCTION MANUAL:
LETTER DESCRIPTIONS
Basic and cursive italic lowercase, pp 32-41
Basic italic capitals, page 42
Cursive italic capitals, page 43
Transition and cursive italic joins, pp 45-49

LETTER DIMENSIONS
Options, page 56
Shape Guidelines, page 57
Size Guidelines, page 58
Slope Guidelines, page 59
Spacing Guidelines, page 60
Speed Guidelines, page 60

ASSESSMENT QUESTIONS
Basic italic lowercase, pp 62-63
Basic italic capitals, page 64
Cursive italic capitals, page 65
Cursive italic lowercase joins, p 66

Happy face shows correct letter or join.

Writing practice for Joins 1 to 8 uses first names with basic italic capitals. As we read and write lowercase approximately 98% of the time, the first attention is on learning lowercase joins.

Cursive capitals come later, pages 50-62. After learning cursive capitals, a student may prefer to use the basic italic capitals with cursive italic lowercase. This is an option if the student feels more comfortable with the plainer capitals. Some like 'the fancier the better' and others prefer 'the simpler the better'.

OPTION available

---

the *Slope Guide* directions to help students maintain an even slope. Messy writing is often due to an uneven slope.

34 Some students will naturally write **v** and **w** pointed at the bottom, while others make them slightly rounded.

36-37 The join out of **r** needs more practice than any other join. If written too fast, the **r** can look like **v**, and **rn** can look like **m**. The **r** has to branch out halfway, touch the waistline, and bend down, THEN join with a short diagonal. It may help if the student uses a "pointed **r**" pausing ever so slightly at the waistline before bending.

37 Important option: Lift after **r**.

44, 75 Place a page of the student's best handwriting in the student's portfolio (student's or teacher's choice).

46 Body height changes to 5mm.

47 Most writing on lined paper will be without a waistline. To create a waistline with notebook paper, see page vi.

48 Begin to gradually increase the speed of writing after all the joins are learned. Use the timed writing on page 77 (INSTRUCTION MANUAL, page 61). Repeat once a month. The *Eyes Closed* exercise is lots of fun and is often a confidence booster.

50-62 The origins of the capital and lowercase letters may be explored further by using the *Development of the Alphabet* in the INSTRUCTION MANUAL, pages 86-93.

65 *The New Reading Teacher's Book of Lists* is a gold mine of information! It lists 338 homophones, 333 homographs, pages of phonograms, and more. The vowel sounds and consonant sounds are also from this book.

68 Line 7 shows an optional join out of **t** into **e**. Show other options, see note for pages 32-33.

72 Make an envelope using decorated paper, colored paper, magazine cover, paper bag, or gift wrap that is at least 8 ½ by 11". Use the envelope pattern on page 108 by duplicating it (or tracing it), placing it over the envelope paper, and cutting around it.

78 For 6mm lines with a capital height, see INSTRUCTION MANUAL, page 102.

76 Students need to know how to read looped cursive. Show them the letters that are the most difficult to read, see INSTRUCTION MANUAL pages 50-51.

From day one, have DESK STRIPS and WALLCHART in place. For extra practice, use BLACKLINE MASTERS. See INSTRUCTION MANUAL, pages 7-8.

BOOK E

GETTY-DUBAY® ITALIC HANDWRITING SERIES – NOTES TO TEACHERS

ASSESSMENT

STEP 1: Direct the student to LOOK at his/her writing and affirm what is the best. Questions are asked requiring a yes/no answer. 'Yes' is affirmation of a task accomplished. 'No' indicates work to be done to improve writing.

STEP 2: Direct the student to PLAN what needs to be improved and how to accomplish this.

STEP 3: Direct the student to put the plan into PRACTICE.

Direct the student to look over a week's writing practice and find a page showing the most improvement. The student then stars the page at the top and tells (teacher or student) how the writing has improved.

Provide the opportunity for each student to select a page of his/her best handwriting to include in the student's portfolio.

Margins contain information, directions, notes, hints, reminders, options, and assessment LOOK, PLAN, PRACTICE.

Trace and copy. Trace dotted model, then copy on lines provided and on lined paper. If needed, also trace solid line model.

NOTE for special attention.

ASSESSMENT

1. LOOK at the writing. Direct the student to circle his/her personal best letter or join. Compare with the models.

2. PLAN: Assist the student in choosing letters that need work to improve the writing. Look at the letter dimensions of shape, size, slope, and spacing. Focus on one at a time. Begin with shape, then size, slope, and spacing. To assess, identify (1) what is going well, (2) what needs to be improved, and (3) what needs to be done to make the improvement. See *IM Assessment*, pages 54-55.

3. PRACTICE writing, making the improvements.

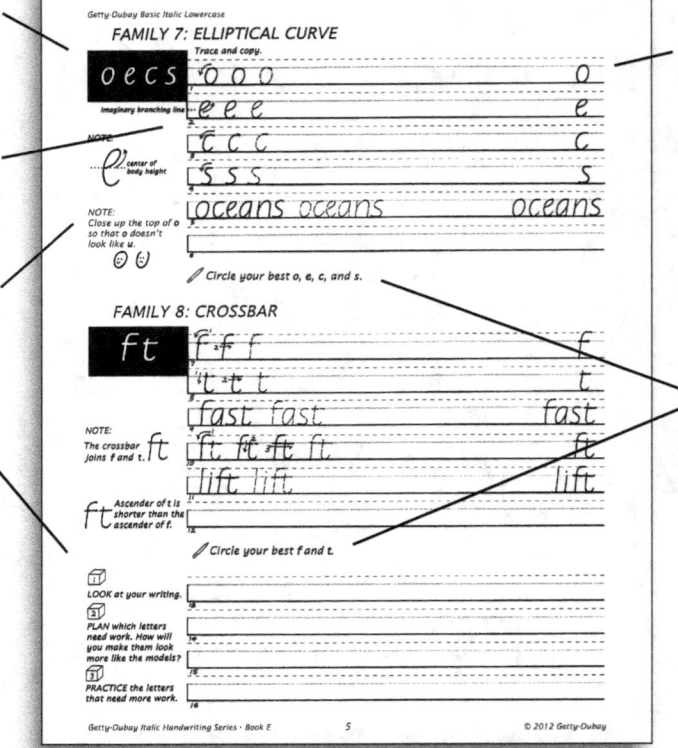

For basic italic the models are also on the right hand side for the left-hander who often covers up the models when he/she writes.

The student circles his/her personal best. It may not be perfect, but it is the best at the moment. Assessment begins with success and affirmation.

PAGES IN BOOK E:

vi-vii *Go over Reminders*, especially Process: pencil positions, paper position, stroke direction and sequence.

2   Pencil picture indicates the student is to circle his/her best letter. Later on, the pencil picture indicates the student is to answer a question by checking "Yes" or "No."

2-7 Review basic italic or introduce basic italic to those new to the program. Ascender and capital height is halfway between the waistline and the line above.

8 Emphasize the importance of basic italic for various purposes. Many times and in many places we are asked to "Please print."

10-11 Transition to lowercase cursive is simple. Keep the same basic letter shapes and add entrance and exit serifs to some letters. Note options.

12-16 Overview of the eight cursive lowercase joins and cursive capitals is provided as an introduction for the student new to italic. May also use a review of joins.

16 Option: basic capitals may be used with cursive lowercase.

17-43 Writing practice for the eight cursive lowercase joins uses words that include vowel sounds, consonant sounds, prefixes, suffixes, and phonograms. Each word is shown using all the possible joins; the join being studied is underlined. Body height is 5mm and 4mm.

18 For major and minor phonograms, see *The New Reading Teacher's Book of Lists*, pages 124-133; also vowel sounds, prefixes, and suffixes.

22 AVOID a scoop and loop. One of the problems with looped cursive is that loops clutter up the letter in exactly the area where the word is read—the top. For example: Can you read this word showing only the tiptop of the capital letters?

Italic keeps the tops of words clean and clear. Loop-free italic is easy to read.

24 The optional join into *n*, *m*, *r*, and *x* comfortable for many students.

25 Place a page of each student's best writing in his/her student portfolio (teacher choice or student choice).

Getty-Dubay® Italic Handwriting Series - Notes to Teachers: BOOK E

CLASSROOM MANAGEMENT
Using direct instruction, present two pages a week, with follow-up practice on lined paper. Allow 20 minutes per page. Demonstrate the process, letter dimensions and assessment for letters and joins. (See pages 14-15.)

Opportunities can be found for further handwriting practice by integrating italic handwriting into other areas of curriculum for 10-15 minutes daily.

PLAN FOR EFFICIENT USE OF DIRECT INSTRUCTION TIME:
1. Students have sharpened pencils on hand.
2. Students have workbooks on hand or a system provided for quick distribution of workbooks (books remain closed until after teacher models letters).
3. Teacher has pre-lined chalkboard or lined transparencies for overhead projector.
4. Teacher writes the page number on chalkboard and models letters.
5. Students write in workbooks.
6. Students and teacher assess writing.

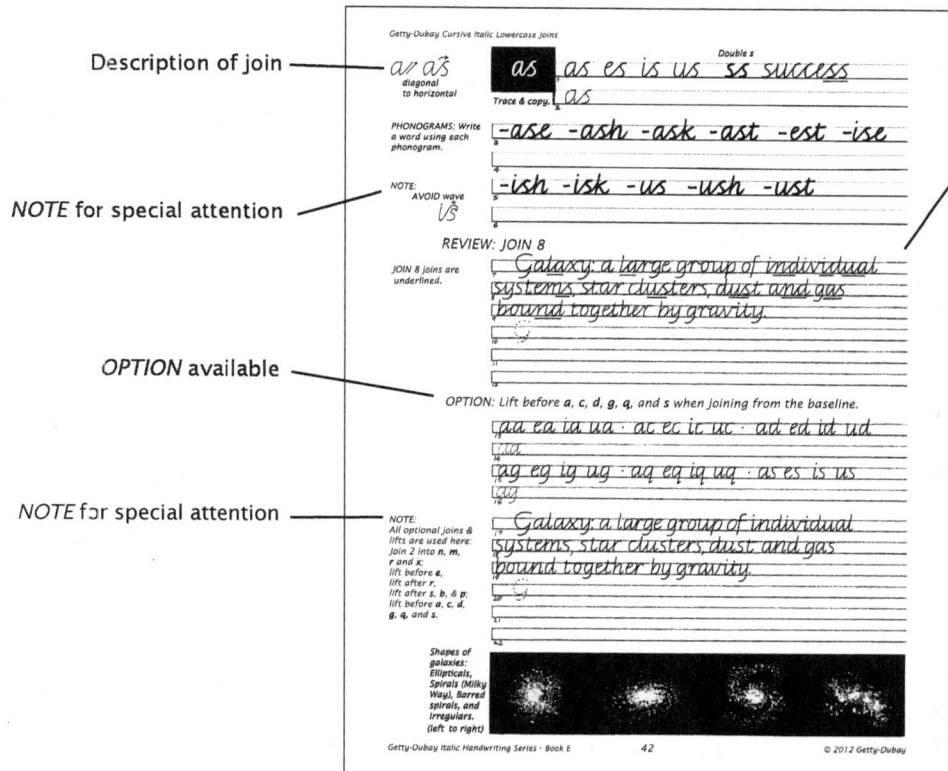

The content for the sentence and paragraph writing practice uses of the six kingdoms of life, DNA, minerals, continents, biomes, planets, our solar system and galaxy.

See INSTRUCTION MANUAL:
LETTER DESCRIPTIONS
Basic and cursive italic lowercase, pp 32-41
Basic italic capitals, page 42
Cursive italic capitals, page 43
Transition and cursive italic joins, pp 45-49

LETTER DIMENSIONS
Options, page 56
Shape Guidelines, page 57
Size Guidelines, page 58
Slope Guidelines, page 59
Spacing Guidelines, page 60
Speed Guidelines, page 60

ASSESSMENT QUESTIONS
Basic italic lowercase, pp 62-63
Basic italic capitals, page 64
Cursive italic capitals, page 65
Cursive italic lowercase joins, p 66

29 Students need to be reminded often not to clench their pencils. They need to relax and not tighten up their hand muscles.

31 and 34 The diagonal join out of *o*, *v*, *w* and *x* into *e* is a modification of the horizontal join.

32-33 Optional joins out of *t* and *f* into *e* are shown, as well as the option to lift after *t* and *f* before *e*. Each student will find the one most comfortable.

35 This is the first time the checklist is shown. Until now, each assessment has centered on one aspect of letter dimensions, such as shape, size, slope, or spacing.

43, 44 Writing with the baseline only is how we write on notebook paper. See page *iv* for a way to get a waistline when using notebook paper.

44, 45 If slope is a problem, now is the time to take care of it. This is the exercise to use. An expanded version of the slope assessment exercise is in the INSTRUCTION MANUAL, page 59. *Timed writing* exercise helps to encourage a gradual increase in the number of words written per minute. Repeat at least once a month.

46-52 Cursive italic capitals use cities of the world as writing practice. For further information about origins of letters, such as Phoenician and Greek letter names, see the *Development of the Alphabet*, INSTRUCTION MANUAL pages 86-93.

There are a few capitals that invite joining out of such as *C*, *K*, and *R*, and perhaps *L* and *Z*. These can join into all letters except *f* and *z*.

53 For envelope pattern, see INSTRUCTION MANUAL page 108.

54 It is important that students be able to read looped cursive. See pages 50-51 in the INSTRUCTION MANUAL for ways to help students recognize other writing styles.

From day one, have DESK STRIPS and WALLCHART in place. For extra practice, use BLACKLINE MASTERS. See INSTRUCTION MANUAL, pages 7-8.

BOOK F

GETTY-DUBAY® ITALIC HANDWRITING SERIES – NOTES TO TEACHERS

ASSESSMENT

STEP 1: Direct the student to LOOK at his/her writing and affirm what is the best. Questions are asked requiring a yes/no answer. 'Yes' is affirmation of a task accomplished. 'No' indicates work to be done to improve writing.

STEP 2: Direct the student to PLAN what needs to be improved and how to accomplish this.

STEP 3: Direct the student to put the plan into PRACTICE.

Direct the student to look over a week's writing practice and find a page showing the most improvement. The student then stars the page at the top and tells (teacher or student) how the writing has improved.

Provide the opportunity for each student to select a page of his/her best handwriting to include in the student's portfolio.

Margins contain information, directions, notes, hints, reminders, options, and assessment LOOK, PLAN, PRACTICE.

NOTE for special attention

ASSESSMENT

1. LOOK at the writing. Direct the student to circle his/her personal best letter or join. Compare with the models.

2. PLAN: Assist the student in choosing letters that need work to improve the writing. Look at the letter dimensions of shape, size, slope, and spacing. Focus on one at a time. Begin with shape, then size, slope, and spacing. To assess, identify (1) what is going well, (2) what needs to be improved, and (3) what needs to be done to make the improvement. See *IM Assessment*, pages 54-55.

3. PRACTICE writing, making the improvements.

The content for the sentence writing practice is word origins, figures of speech, word groups, and word entertainment.

Origins of the alphabet include Egyptian hieroglyphs, Phoenician letters and names, Greek letters and names, and Roman letters.

PAGES IN BOOK F:

vi-vii Go over *Reminders*, especially Process: pencil position, paper position, stroke direction, and sequence.

2 Pencil picture means "circle" or answer "yes/no".

2-7 Use these pages as a review of basic italic lowercase and capitals. If a student is new to the program, spend more time on this introduction to the italic letter shapes.

8 Word origins begin here with acronyms written in basic italic. Small capitals are used to introduce word origins, words, word groups, and word entertainment. Small capitals are the same height as the lowercase body height. Body height changes to 4mm on this page.

10-16 Use these pages as a review of Transition and the eight cursive italic joins. If a student is new to the program, spend more time on this introduction to the cursive italic.

17-43 Writing practice using the eight cursive italic joins includes two letter combinations, words, and sentences. The words use vowel sounds, consonant sounds, prefixes, suffixes, double letter, silent letter, initial consonant blends, and phonograms to practice each join. The sentence content includes word origins, figures of speech, word groups, and word entertainment.

Getty-Dubay® Italic Handwriting Series · Instruction Manual   28   © 2013 Getty-Dubay

Getty-Dubay® Italic Handwriting Series - Notes to Teachers: BOOK F

CLASSROOM MANAGEMENT
Using direct instruction, present two pages a week, with follow-up practice on lined paper. Allow 20 minutes per page. Demonstrate the process, letter dimensions and assessment for letters and joins (see pages 14-15).

Opportunities can be found for further handwriting practice by integrating italic handwriting into other areas of curriculum for 10-15 minutes daily.

PLAN FOR EFFICIENT USE OF DIRECT INSTRUCTION TIME:
1. Students have sharpened pencils on hand.
2. Students have workbooks on hand or a system provided for quick distribution of workbooks (books remain closed until after teacher models letters).
3. Teacher has pre-lined chalkboard or lined transparencies for overhead projector.
4. Teacher writes the page number on chalkboard and models letters.
5. Students write in workbooks.
6. Students and teacher assess writing.

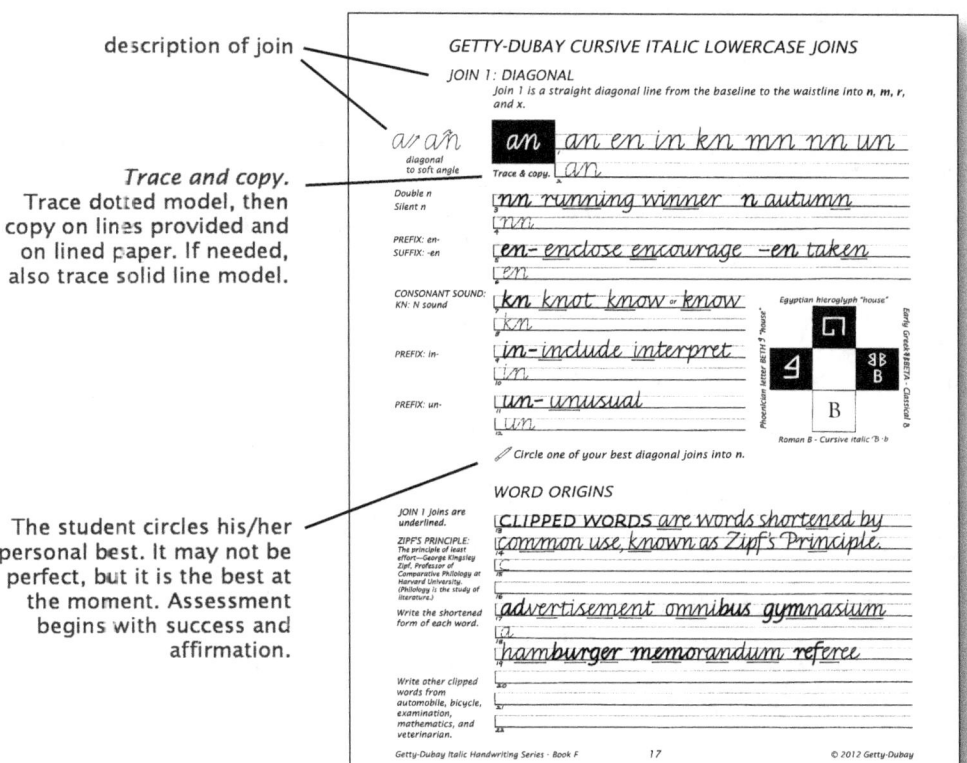

description of join

Trace and copy. Trace dotted model, then copy on lines provided and on lined paper. If needed, also trace solid line model.

The student circles his/her personal best. It may not be perfect, but it is the best at the moment. Assessment begins with success and affirmation.

See INSTRUCTION MANUAL:

LETTER DESCRIPTIONS
Basic and cursive italic lowercase, pages 32-41
Basic italic capitals, page 42
Cursive italic capitals, page 43
Transition and cursive italic joins, pages 45-49

LETTER DIMENSIONS
Options, page 56
Shape Guidelines, page 57
Size Guidelines, page 58
Slope Guidelines, page 59
Spacing Guidelines, page 60
Speed Guidelines, page 60

ASSESSMENT QUESTIONS
Basic italic lowercase, pp. 62-63
Basic italic capitals, page 64
Cursive italic capitals, page 65
Cursive italic lowercase joins, p. 66

Word origins include: acronyms and initializations, compound words, contractions, onomatopoeia, portmanteau words, and Zipf's Principle or clipped words.
Words include: homographs, homophones, synomyms, and antonyms.
Word groups include: analogies, euphemisms, hyperbole, idiomatic expressions, maxims, metaphors, mnemonics, oxymoron, proverbs, and similies.
Word entertainment include: alliteration, palindromes, pangrams, polysyllabic profundities, rebus, rhopalic sentences, Tom Swifties, and Spoonerisms.
See page 44 for *Timed Writing* exercise or page 61, INSTRUCTION MANUAL. Do this exercise once a month. For a student with an uneven letter slope use the *Slope Assessment* exercise on page 59, INSTRUCTION MANUAL.

45-49 Cursive capitals include origins of the alphabet. Names of First Nation tribes and communities of North America are used for writing practice.

53 Use this for special holiday or gift projects. Other projects, including a hand-sewn book, a letter/booklet, and an envelope template are in the INSTRUCTION MANUAL, pages 81-85 and 108.

55-56 Lines including capital height are found in the INSTRUCTION MANUAL, pages 102-104.

Assessment checklist:

CHECKLIST
____ *letter shape*
____ *letter size*
____ *letter slope*
____ *letter spacing*

From day one, have DESK STRIPS and WALLCHART in place. For extra practice, use BLACKLINE MASTERS. See INSTRUCTION MANUAL, pages 7-8.

BOOK G

GETTY-DUBAY® ITALIC HANDWRITING SERIES – NOTES TO TEACHERS

BOOK G is specifically designed as a self-instruction workbook and begins with an overview of basic italic, a print script, then presents a total cursive handwriting program. Paragraphs acquainting the student with a brief history of the origins of our letters are used as the writing practice for both basic and cursive italic. This is the only book in the series with information on writing with the edged pen.

ASSESSMENT (for classroom use if not using workbook as an independent text)
STEP 1: Direct the student to LOOK at his/her writing and affirm what is the best. Answer questions with 'Yes' to affirm task accomplished or 'No' to indicate work to be done to improve handwriting.
STEP 2: Direct the student to PLAN what needs to be improved and how to accomplish this.
STEP 3: Direct the student to put the plan into PRACTICE.

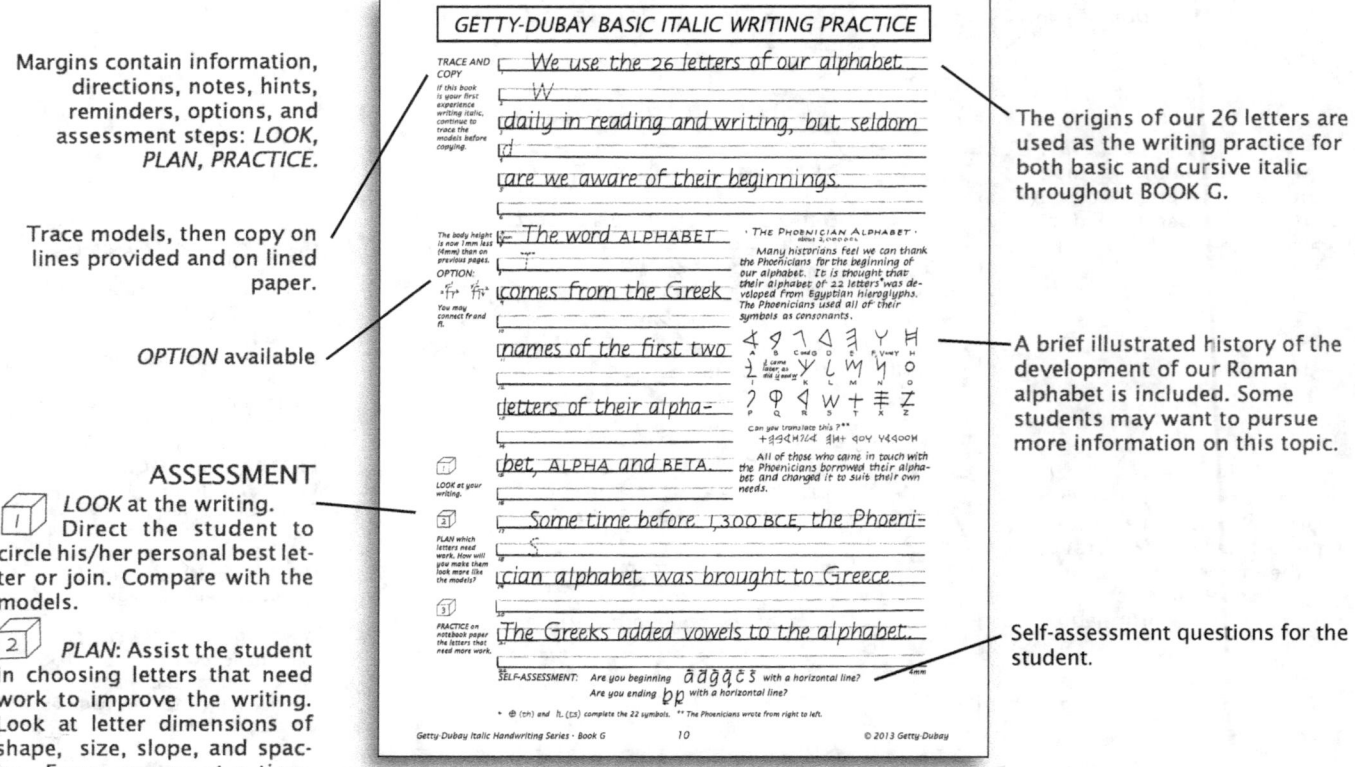

Margins contain information, directions, notes, hints, reminders, options, and assessment steps: LOOK, PLAN, PRACTICE.

Trace models, then copy on lines provided and on lined paper.

OPTION available

The origins of our 26 letters are used as the writing practice for both basic and cursive italic throughout BOOK G.

A brief illustrated history of the development of our Roman alphabet is included. Some students may want to pursue more information on this topic.

Self-assessment questions for the student.

ASSESSMENT

1. LOOK at the writing. Direct the student to circle his/her personal best letter or join. Compare with the models.

2. PLAN: Assist the student in choosing letters that need work to improve the writing. Look at letter dimensions of shape, size, slope, and spacing. Focus on one at a time. Begin with shape, then size, slope, and spacing. To assess, identify (1) what is going well, (2) what needs to be improved, and (3) what needs to be done to make the improvement. See Assessment, pages 54-55.

3. PRACTICE writing, making the improvements.

PAGES IN BOOK G International Edition:

vi-vii *Go over Reminders*, especially Process: pencil positions, paper position, stroke direction and sequence.

2 Pencil picture indicates the student is to circle his/her best letter. Later on, the pencil picture indicates the student is to answer a question by checking "Yes" or "No."

2-3 As an introduction to italic or as a review, letter are presented at a 9mm body height to help student focus on letter shapes, tool hold, and hand movements.

9 See @ on line 17. History of @: Latin word ad for "at".

$$a + \partial = @$$

10-11 Emphasize the importance of basic italic for many purposes: filling out forms, signs and posters, lists, applications, etc. Often we are asked to "Please print."

13-14 Important handwriting tips to improve legibility.

18 See capital **Y** options.

28 Transition to cursive italic retains the same basic italic letter shapes and adds entrance and exit serifs. (Only **k** changes from two strokes to one stroke.)

21-31 The 8 joins are presented as an introduction or as a review. Remind students to trace the models.

23 Optional joins begin on this page. Encourage students to try the standard join and the option, then select the one that is most comfortable to write.

38 Use the timed writing to help students increase speed. Repeat timed writings as often as time allows.

Getty-Dubay® Italic Handwriting Series - Notes to Teachers: BOOK G

Direct student to look over a week's writing practice and find a page showing the most improvement. The student then stars the page at the top and tells the teacher or fellow student how the writing has improved. On a weekly basis, have each student save a page of "personal best" writing in the student's portfolio.

CLASSROOM MANAGEMENT
Using direct instruction, present two pages a week, with follow-up practice on lined paper. Demonstrate the process, letter dimensions, and assessment for letters and joins. (See pages 14-15.)

Integrate italic handwriting into other areas of the curriculum daily.

Joins 1-8 are presented step-by-step to provide the writer with a legible cursive italic hand.

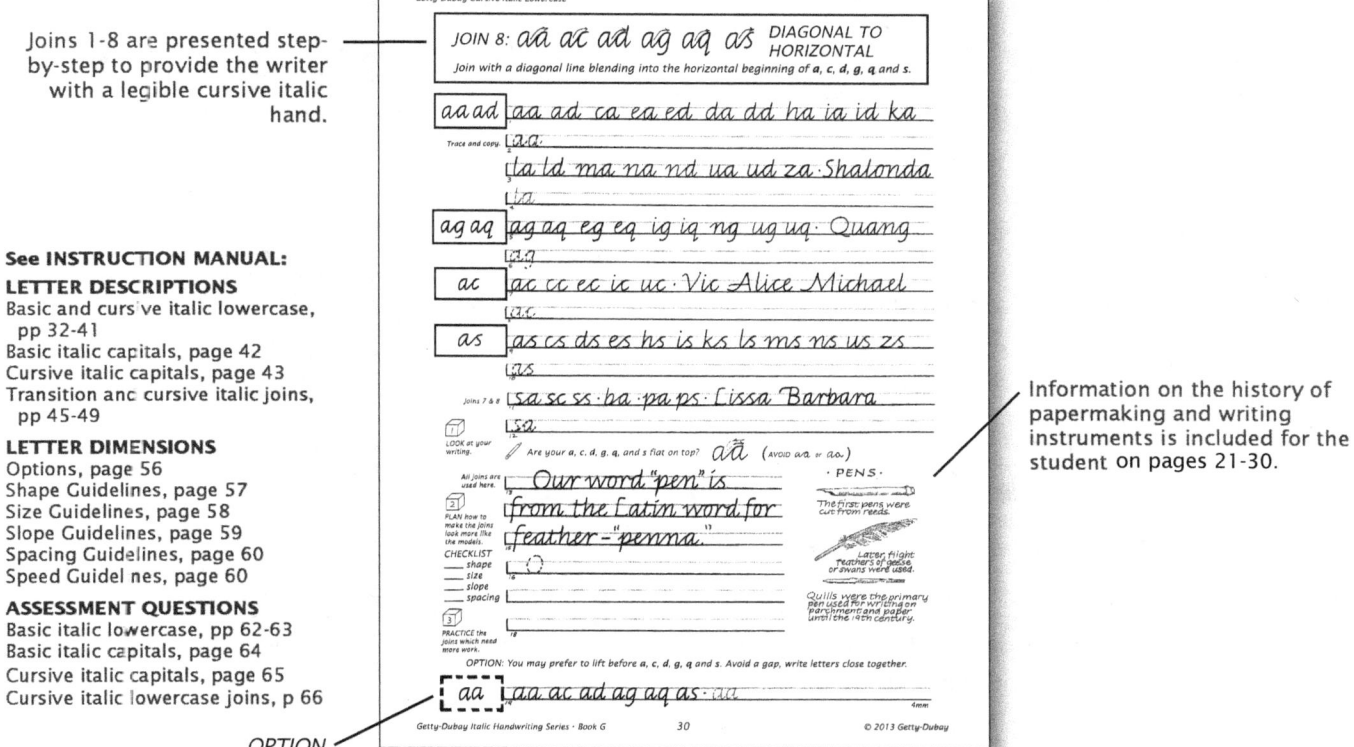

See INSTRUCTION MANUAL:
LETTER DESCRIPTIONS
Basic and cursive italic lowercase, pp 32-41
Basic italic capitals, page 42
Cursive italic capitals, page 43
Transition and cursive italic joins, pp 45-49

LETTER DIMENSIONS
Options, page 56
Shape Guidelines, page 57
Size Guidelines, page 58
Slope Guidelines, page 59
Spacing Guidelines, page 60
Speed Guidelines, page 60

ASSESSMENT QUESTIONS
Basic italic lowercase, pp 62-63
Basic italic capitals, page 64
Cursive italic capitals, page 65
Cursive italic lowercase joins, p 66

OPTION

Information on the history of papermaking and writing instruments is included for the student on pages 21-30.

40 *Spacing* and *Speed Guidelines* are presented.

41-55 These pages present an introduction to italic handwriting with the edged pen. This section may be completed with the standard pencil or pen for extra practice, but the chisel-edged writing instrument will add a new look to the letter forms.

Besides metal fountain and dip nib pens, a student (and the teacher) can enhance the written message by cutting and writing with a popsicle stick, tongue depressor, or cattail stalk as shown on page 42. This method of writing with an edged pen becomes an art form and can be expanded on with your students—and exciting area to explore!

56 Ways students can enhance their letter writing and accompanying envelopes are shown.

60 If a student has difficulty maintaining a consistent letter slope, these slope lines may be reproduced and positioned under his/her notebook paper.

61-62 For 5mm and 4mm ruled lines with capital height, see INSTRUCTION MANUAL, pp 103-104.

From day one, have DESK STRIPS and WALLCHART in place. For extra practice, use BLACKLINE MASTERS. See INSTRUCTION MANUAL, pages 7- 8.

PLAN FOR EFFICIENT USE OF DIRECT INSTRUCTION TIME:

1. Students have sharpened pencils on hand.

2. Students have workbooks on hand or a system provided for quick distribution of workbooks (books remain closed until after teacher models letters).

3. Teacher has pre-lined chalkboard or lined transparencies for overhead projector.

4. Teacher writes the page number on chalkboard and models letters.

5. Students write in workbooks.

6. Students and teacher assess writing.

GETTY-DUBAY® ITALIC HANDWRITING SERIES
LETTER DESCRIPTIONS: LOWERCASE FAMILY 1

BASIC ITALIC **CURSIVE ITALIC**

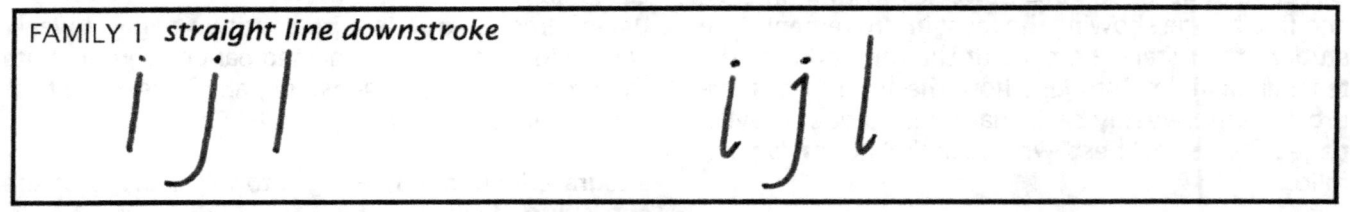

SIZE, SHAPE OF LETTERS AND STROKE SEQUENCE:
Maintain a consistent letter slope of 0°–15° to the right. Models are written at 5° slope.

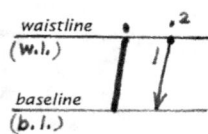 From waistline move downward to baseline. Complete letter with dot. One pencil lift. Tell beginning student to "bump" the baseline. Two stroke letter, one lift.

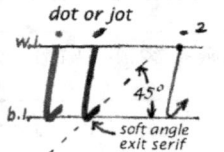 Letter remains same as basic form except curve upward at baseline to complete first stroke using a soft angle exit serif.
OPTION: dot or jot. (The jot may be faster to execute during rapid writing.)

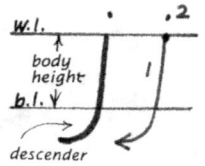 From waistline move downward below baseline, curving left, (do not curve upward at end of stroke). Dot. Two stroke letter, one lift.

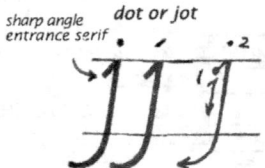 Letter remains same as basic form except begin stroke 1 with sharp entrance serif. Stroke 1 touches waistline but does not go above.
OPTION: dot or jot. (The jot may be faster to execute during rapid writing.)

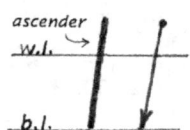 Beginning above waistline, move downward to baseline. One stroke letter, no lift.

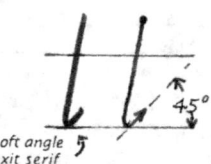 Letter remains same as basic form except curve upward at a 45° angle to form exit serif.

Ascenders and descenders are ¹/₂ body height.

SLOPE: Letter slope is the slant of a letter. A slight letter slope to the right of the vertical of approximately 5°–12° is generally considered acceptable for italic. But a slope from 0°–15° may be used.

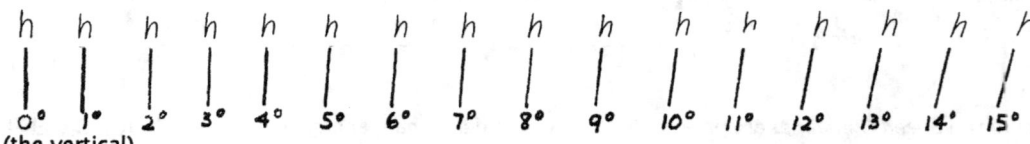

The degree of letter slope is important, but consistency is more important. The workbooks provide consistent models, and the student should be encouraged to find a comfortable slope and maintain it as well as he/she is able. For the student just learning to write, correct letter shape and size are more important than letter slope. Do help the student who slopes letters to the left, "backhand." Have the student shift the paper by swinging the bottom of page farther right for either the left- or right-handed writer.

SPACING: There are three widths of spacing letters in words:

1. Wide space between straight line downstrokes

2. Medium space between straight line and curve

3. Narrow space between two curves at the center
Narrow space between diagonal and downstroke at the waistline

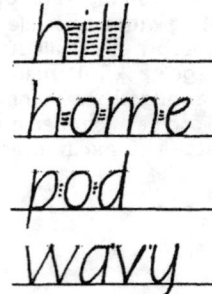

Getty-Dubay® Italic Handwriting Series – Letter Descriptions: Lowercase Family 1

OBJECTIVES: The student traces each letter or partial form and completes each partial letter on the student page. In Books A, B and C, student writes his/her own letters at each given dot, or in the blank spaces, and understands the dot, when used, is a beginning point and NOT part of the letter.

EVALUATION: j is used as an example, but similar problems may occur with i and l. Here are some differences that may cause illegibility:

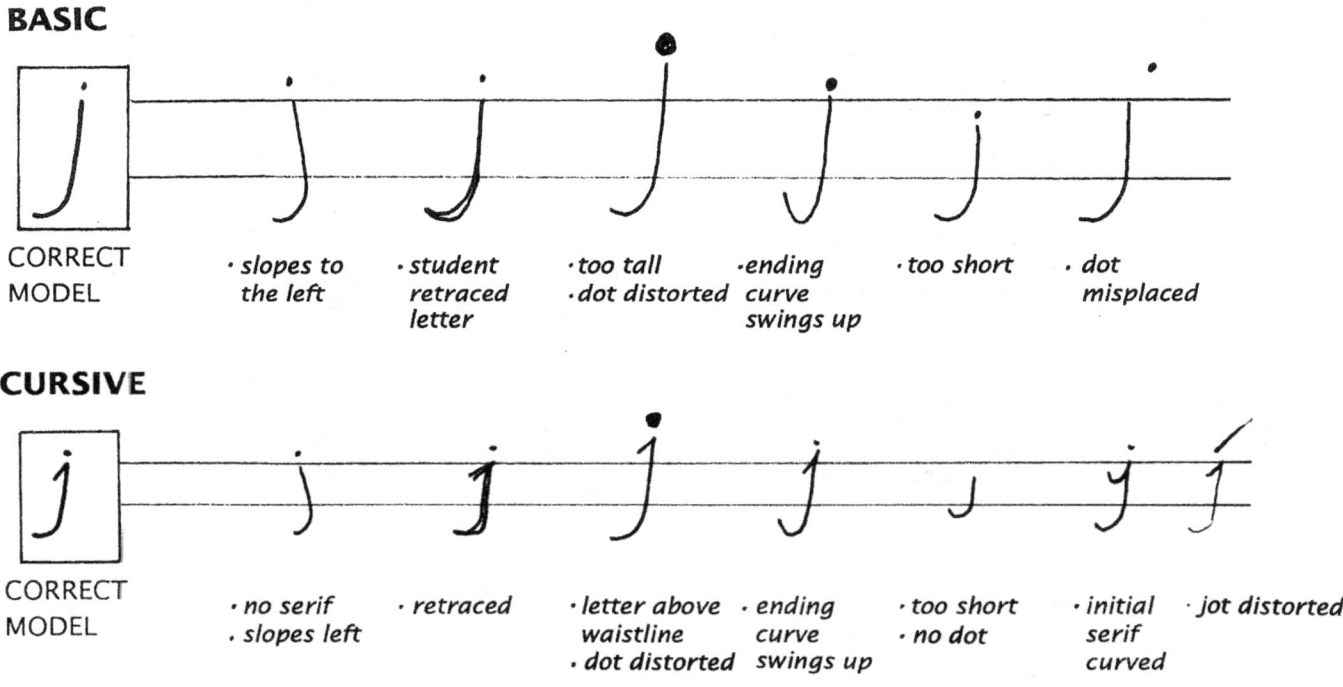

BASIC

CORRECT MODEL
- slopes to the left
- student retraced letter
- too tall
- dot distorted
- ending curve swings up
- too short
- dot misplaced

CURSIVE

CORRECT MODEL
- no serif
- slopes left
- retraced
- letter above waistline
- dot distorted
- ending curve swings up
- too short
- no dot
- initial serif curved
- jot distorted

To help student self-evaluate his/her work, ask student to compare the letter with model on the page, and to tell you about one or more things that differ from the model.

ACTIVITY: (Suitable for any letter) ▪ suggested for grades K–2.
Using a jump rope*, student or instructor forms a letter on the floor. Student skips or walks alongside of the rope in proper stroke sequence. Tape colored circle to floor for dot on **i** and **j**. This idea may be used as a relay game. (Use same letter for each team.)
*Use two ropes for two stroke letters, **k**, etc. Use long, two-person rope for some or all letters.

Children have more need of models than of critics JOUBERT 1754-1824

GETTY-DUBAY® ITALIC HANDWRITING SERIES
LETTER DESCRIPTIONS: LOWERCASE FAMILY 2

BASIC ITALIC **CURSIVE ITALIC**

FAMILY 2 *diagonal line*

k v w x z   k or k v w x z
              OPTION

SIZE, SHAPE OF LETTERS AND STROKE SEQUENCE:
Maintain consistent letter slope of 0°–15° to the right. Models are written at 5° slope.

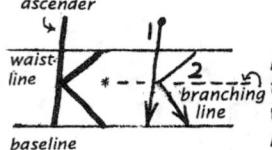

1. Move downward and touch baseline. 2. From waistline, angle left to touch stroke 1 halfway between waistline and baseline. Then angle right to baseline.
Two stroke letter, one lift.

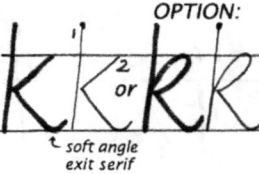

k remains the same except for soft angle exit serif.
OPTION: k may be a one-stroke letter. Move downward to baseline, retrace stroke to branching line, form curve by moving up to waistline, curve around and close at branching line; then angle right to baseline, then up to right to form exit serif.

From waistline angle right to baseline, touch, then angle right to waistline.
One stroke letter, no lift.

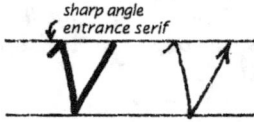

v remains the same except for sharp entrance serif. Slightly below waistline move upward to right, touch waistline, angle sharply downward to the right to baseline, then up to waistline.

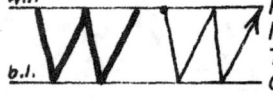

From waistline angle right to baseline, angle right up to waistline. Then repeat.
One stroke letter, no lift.

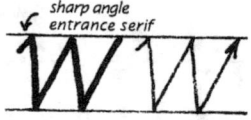

w also remains same except for sharp entrance serif. See V above.

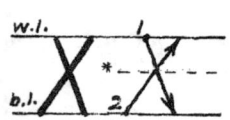

From waistline angle right to baseline. Lift. From baseline angle right to waistline, crossing stroke one at branching line, which is halfway between waistline and baseline.
Two stroke letter, one lift.

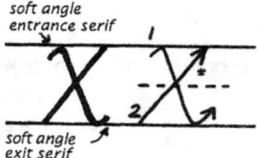

x remains same except for serifs. A B serifs are steep angles.

At waistline move right horizontally, angle from waistline left downward to baseline, then move horizontally to the right on the baseline.
One stroke letter, no lift.

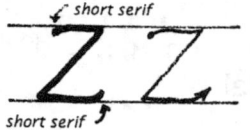

z remains same except begin with slight serif and end with a slight serif.

Ascenders and descenders are ¹/₂ body height.

*Branching line is an imaginary line at a point halfway between waistline and baseline. When demonstrating letterforms, discuss and write in branching line as shown above.

SLOPE: The axis of the letters **v**, **w**, and **x** follow letter slope.

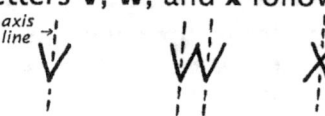

Check left points of **z** to determine letter slope.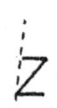

SPACING: Letters are written close together. Leave about the width of lowercase **n** between words if the student has mastered the writing of the alphabet. Beginners may need two of their own small fingers between words to assist in the reading and writing process. In that event, furnish the left-handed young person with a strip of cardboard the proper width to measure space between words. Left-handed student can't use the right-hand fingers to space with while writing!

Getty-Dubay® Italic Handwriting Series – Letter Descriptions: Lowercase Family 2

OBJECTIVES: The student traces each letter or partial form and completes each partial letter on the student page. Student writes own letters at each given dot (Books A, B and C) or in the blank spaces provided. Student understands the arrow indicates direction of the stroke and that dot is a beginning point, NOT part of the letter. Student traces word and sentence models, then writes his/her own in spaces provided during* or after instructor gives instructions orally and visually.

*Generally students write in workbooks AFTER instructions are given.

EVALUATION: Student self-evaluation— student circles one, two or three "best" letters on workbook page, or "best" word.
Difference that may cause illegibility:

BASIC

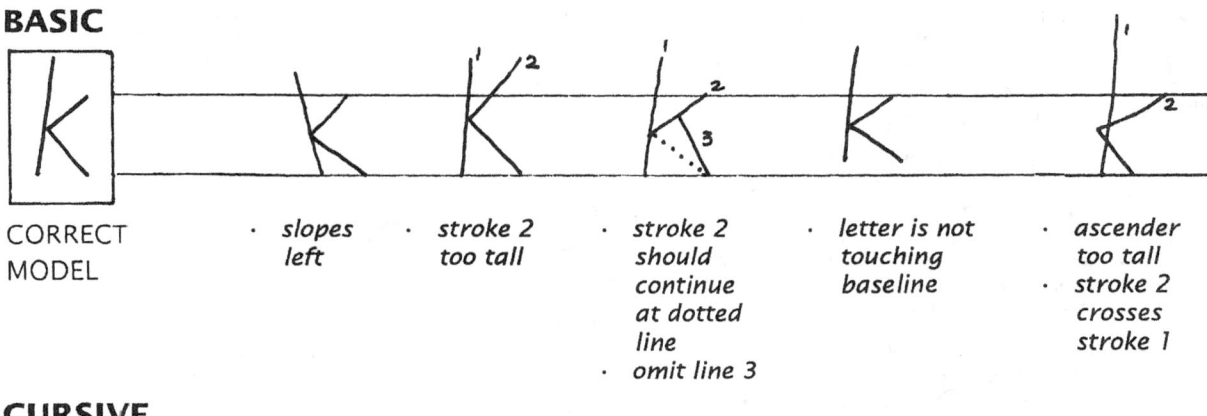

CORRECT MODEL
- slopes left
- stroke 2 too tall
- stroke 2 should continue at dotted line
- omit line 3
- letter is not touching baseline
- ascender too tall
- stroke 2 crosses stroke 1

CURSIVE

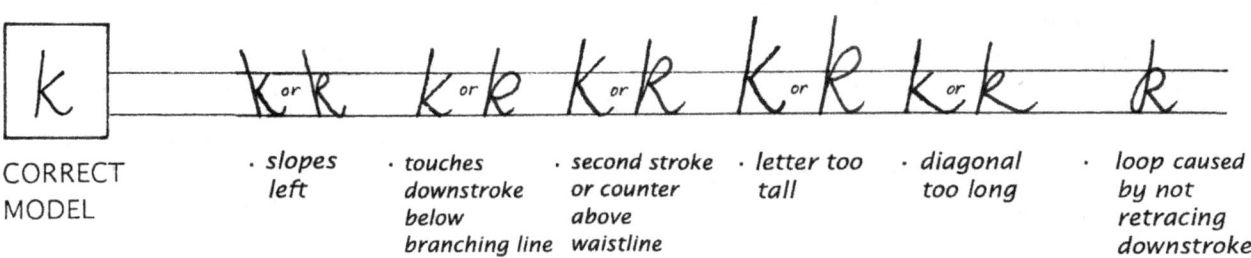

CORRECT MODEL
- slopes left
- touches downstroke below branching line
- second stroke or counter above waistline
- letter too tall
- diagonal too long
- loop caused by not retracing downstroke

ACTIVITY: (suitable for any letter, letters, words, short sentences) Student folds sheet of paper "corner to corner,"* then corner to corner a second time. Folds form four writing spaces. Student writes letters, words and/or sentences in spaces.

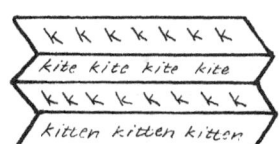

*corner to corner - the words "corner to corner" are used in assisting the young person (Grades Kg-3) fold paper accurately. When demonstrating how to match corners AB/CD, say, "Fold your paper corner to corner."

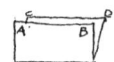

This same paper fold works with adults for those who want to learn to write on a straight line without a lined sheet. Write in the middle of each space, using the folds as visual guidelines. Use with or without edged pen.

· To Teach is to Learn ·

GETTY-DUBAY® ITALIC HANDWRITING SERIES
LETTER DESCRIPTIONS: LOWERCASE FAMILIES 3 & 4

BASIC ITALIC   **CURSIVE ITALIC**

FAMILY 3 *arch* • FAMILY 4 *inverted arch*

hmnr·uy   hmnr·uy

SIZE, SHAPE, OF LETTERS AND STROKE SEQUENCE:
Maintain consistent letter slope of 0–15° to the right. Models are written at 5° slope.

CLOCKWISE CURVE

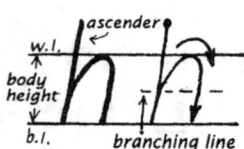

Begin above waistline, move downward to baseline, retrace upward to branching line, branch upward to right, touch waistline, complete arch by curving downward; move down to baseline.
One stroke letter, no pencil lift.

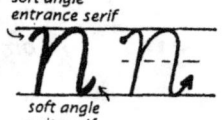

Letter remains same except for addition of exit serif.
Roll into exit serif, not ↳.
Be sure to swing serif upward at about a 45° angle to the writing line. See **h** illustration.

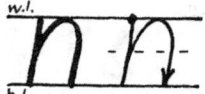

From waistline move downward to baseline, retrace upward to branching line, branch upward to right, touch waistline, complete arch by curving downward, move down to baseline; repeat to form second arch.
One stroke letter, no lift.

Letter remains same except for entrance and exit serifs.
roll into entrance serif   roll out of exit serif

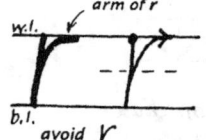

From waistline move to baseline, retrace upward to branching line, branch upward to the right, touch waistline, complete arch by curving downward, move down to baseline.
One stroke letter, no lift.

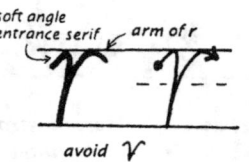

Letter remains same except for entrance and exit serifs.

From waistline move to baseline, retrace upward to branching line, branch upward to the right to waistline, then move along horizontal of waistline a very short distance.
One stroke letter, no lift.

Basic italic *r* arm extends horizontally to right →.(Cursive form with downward curving arm confuses the very young learner.) Cursive *r* has entrance serif and arm that curves downward to accommodate join out of r: *m, rv*

COUNTERCLOCKWISE CURVE

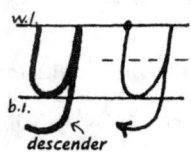

From waistline move downward; curve right, touching baseline, curve upward to branching line; move up to waistline, then straight down to baseline at a proper (0°–15°) letter slope. One stroke letter, no lift.

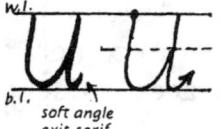

Letter remains same except exit serif.

From waistline move downward; curve right, touching baseline, curve upward to branching line; move up to waistline, then down below baseline, curving left to complete letter. One stroke, no lift.

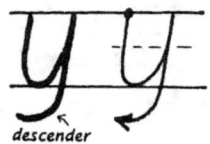

Letter remains same.

Ascenders and descenders are 1/2 body height.

BRANCHING: The letters k, x, h, m, n, r, u, y, a, d, g, q, b, p and e (15 out of 26), incorporate the use of the branching line in some manner.

A NOTE about **m** and **n**: One way to introduce these written letters and the sounds the letters stand for is as shown: 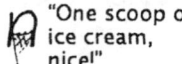 "One scoop of ice cream, nice!"   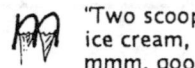 "Two scoops of ice cream, mmm, good!"

Getty-Dubay® Italic Handwriting Series – Letter Descriptions: Lowercase Families 3 & 4

OBJECTIVES: The student traces each letter or partial form and completes each partial letter on the student page. Student writes own letters at each given dot or in the blank spaces provided. Student understands the arrow indicates direction of the stroke and that the dot is a beginning point, not part of the letter. Student traces word and sentence models, then writes his/her own words and sentences in spaces provided during* or after instructor gives directions orally and visually. *usually AFTER!

EVALUATION: Student analyzes own letter forms* for shape, size, slope, spacing and direction strokes are being written. One week emphasize evaluation of shape of the letters, the next week size, etc. Say to the student, "How is your letter different from the one printed in your book?" Let student discover differences if he/she is able. Avoid saying the student's letter is WRONG; it is not wrong, it's DIFFERENT. You can help students feel good about their handwriting!

* according to student's age and ability

BASIC

| CORRECT MODEL | · ascender too short | · branches from baseline instead of branching line | · slopes left (If student is left-handed, correct the paper position.) | · final downstroke not on base line | · too wide · dot is not part of the letter | · arch above waistline |

CURSIVE

| CORRECT MODEL | · slopes left · ascender too tall | · serif distorted | · serif horizontal | · arch is above waistline | · branches from baseline instead of branching line | · loop in ascender |

ACTIVITY: Ask students to make a letter family book out of long paper scraps.* Depending on ability and age level of students, they will write letters, words, sentences and/or paragraphs incorporating the letters of a particular family or families.
*Need scraps? See a print shop in your area. They may have some for your students.

Students may illustrate booklet too!

All words are pegs to hang ideas on
HENRY WARD BEECHER

GETTY-DUBAY® ITALIC HANDWRITING SERIES
LETTER DESCRIPTIONS: LOWERCASE FAMILIES 5 & 6

BASIC ITALIC   **CURSIVE ITALIC**

FAMILY 5 *basic a shape* • FAMILY 6 *inverted basic a shape*

adgq·bp   *adgq·bp*

SIZE, SHAPE OF LETTERS & STROKE SEQUENCE:
Maintain a consistent letter slope of 0°–15° to the right. Models are written at 5° slope.

COUNTERCLOCKWISE CURVE   COUNTERCLOCKWISE CURVE

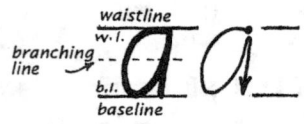 Move left horizontally, curve downward to the baseline, curve upward to branching line, move up to waistline; move downward at letter slope to baseline.

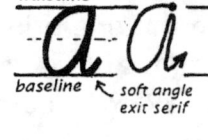 Letter remains same as basic italic except for exit serif. Curve up at about a 45° angle to baseline.

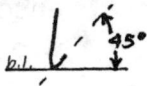

 Move left horizontally curving downward to baseline, curve upward to branching line, move up to waistline, and beyond waistline; move downward to baseline.

 Letter remains same as basic italic except for exit serif. Curve up to form serif at about a 45° angle to the baseline.

 Move left horizontally, curve down to baseline, curve up to branching line, then up to waistline.; move downward below baseline, curving left to complete letter.

 Letter remains same as basic italic.

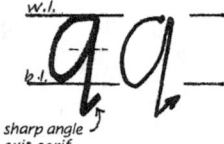 Move left horizontally, curve down to baseline, curve up to branching line, then up to waistline; move downward below baseline; finish with sharp upward serif.

 Letter remains same as basic italic.

All 6 letters are one stroke, no pencil lift.

CLOCKWISE CURVE   CLOCKWISE CURVE

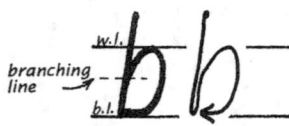 From above waistline, move downward to baseline, move upward to branching line, branch upward to waistline, then downward in an elliptical curve; close horizontally on baseline.

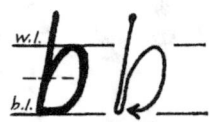 Letter remains same as basic italic.

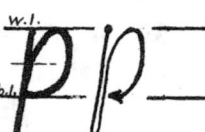 From waistline, move down below baseline, then back up to branching line; branch upward to waistline, then downward in an elliptical curve; close horizontally on baseline.

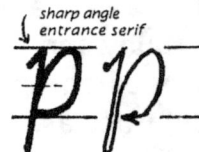 Letter remains same as basic form except begin slightly below waistline, angle up to waistline, then downward to form sharp angle entrance serif.

BRANCHING: The branching line is an imaginary line that may be drawn in for demonstration purposes when introducing and reviewing the 15 letters listed: k, x, h, m, n, r, u, y, a, d, g, q, b, p and e. All of the letters above involve the branching line.

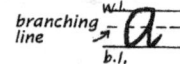 "... from baseline, curve up to branching line, then move up to waistline, ..."

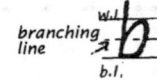 "Move down to baseline, up to branching line; branch away from stem up to waistline, ..."

Getty-Dubay® Italic Handwriting Series – Letter Descriptions: Lowercase Families 5 & 6

OBJECTIVES: The student traces each letter or partial form and completes each partial letter on student page (Books A,B). In Book A, student writes more letters (or words if student is reading) and/or draws pictures in blank space provided at lower left of page. Student writes his/her own letters at each given dot in Books A, B and C, or in blank spaces. The student understands the dot, when used, is a beginning point and NOT part of the letter. The student understands arrows indicate direction of strokes. Student can name stroke sequences and letter parts.

EVALUATION SUGGESTIONS: Review vocabulary at each presentation as you demonstrate letters, words, sentences, e.g., waistline, baseline, branching, letter slope. Student evaluates own letterforms by comparing them with models in workbook. Are letters close together, far apart? Letter slope consistent? Counters consistent in width?  The letters h, n, u, y, b, p, a, d, g, q, o have counters of equal width.

Assist student in finding differences between own letters and models.

BASIC

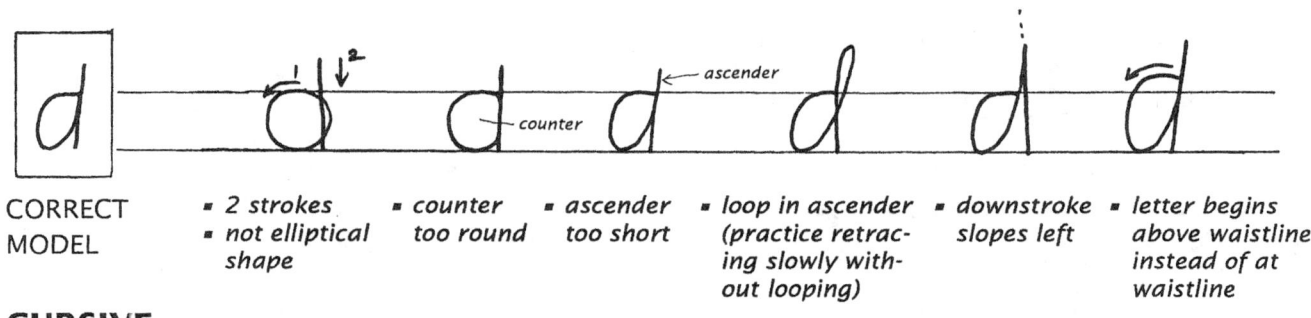

CORRECT MODEL
- 2 strokes
- not elliptical shape
- counter too round
- ascender too short
- loop in ascender (practice retracing slowly without looping)
- downstroke slopes left
- letter begins above waistline instead of at waistline

CURSIVE

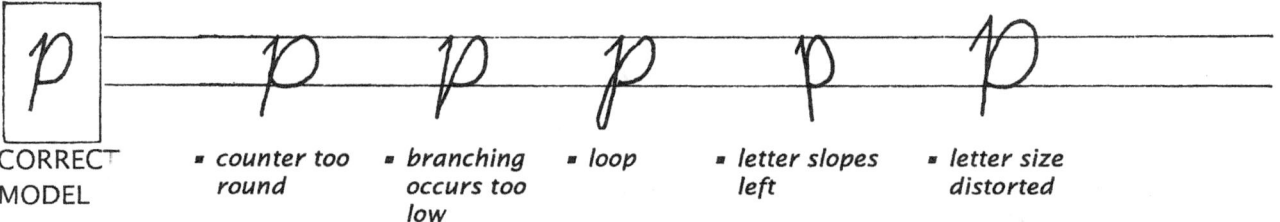

CORRECT MODEL
- counter too round
- branching occurs too low
- loop
- letter slopes left
- letter size distorted

ACTIVITY: After letters introduced, make small book* as follow-up, or complete as spring project.

Two or three times a week, complete a page as a letter review, vocabulary builder, etc. FOR BOOK: run 7 sheets of 8 ½" x 14" ditto paper - lines usually show through for use on both sides. First page can be title page. Cut construction cover 9"x 15" (23 x 38 cms). Stitch. Decorate cover. Be sure to begin aA on right hand page. Sixth graders have fun making elaborate books!

> *I hear and I forget,*
> *I see and I remember,*   ORIENTAL WISDOM
> *I do and I understand*

*For small book stitching directions, see p.80. If possible, have older student help Kg & Gr. 1 student.

GETTY-DUBAY® ITALIC HANDWRITING SERIES
LETTER DESCRIPTIONS: LOWERCASE FAMILIES 7 & 8

BASIC ITALIC

FAMILY 7 *elliptical curve*

o e c s

CURSIVE ITALIC

o e c s ns ns   OPTIONS:

Letters remain the same as basic italic.   **Join 3**   **Join 8**

SIZE, SHAPE & STROKE SEQUENCE
COUNTERCLOCKWISE LETTERS

From waistline, curve downward counterclockwise, touch baseline, curve upward overlapping beginning point to form an ellipse.
One stroke letter, no lift.

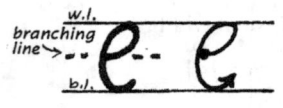

At branching line curve upward to waistline in a counterclockwise motion, touching waistline; curve downward to baseline; continue to curve upward counterclockwise to end. One stroke letter, no lift.

or alternate 2-stroke e   see p. 47

At waistline move left horizontally, curve downward counterclockwise to baseline; curve up about ¼ of total space between waistline and baseline.
One stroke letter, no lift.

At waistline move left horizontally; curve downward counterclockwise, then clockwise; touch baseline; curve up slightly.
One stroke letter, no lift.

NOTES ON SPACING

Generally two downstrokes have the most distance between:

ll hill hill

A downstroke and a curve are closer:

lc log log

And generally two curves are the closest:

)(look look

These rules work most but not all of the time. But don't spend much time with rules—spacing is done by the eye and the hand!

JOIN OPTIONS:

Join 3   s ns   Join 3: When joining from baseline top of s is omitted.

Join 8   s ns   Join 8: When joining from baseline top of s remains the same.

FAMILY 8 *crossbar*

f t

f t

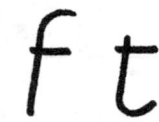

Begin above waistline, move horizontally left, curve; move downward to baseline. Stroke two: at left of stroke one, on or just below waistline, move horizontally to a point directly below beginning of stroke one.
Two stroke letter, one lift.

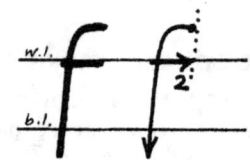

Letter remains same as basic italic, except stroke one moves downward below baseline.

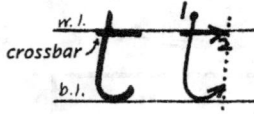

Lowercase **t** is a SHORT letter. Begin slightly above waistline, move downward, curving right just before baseline; touch baseline, curve up to complete letter. Stroke two: at left of stroke one, on or just below waistline, move horizontally to a point directly above ending of stroke one.
Two stroke letter, one lift.

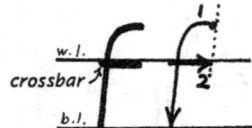

Letter remains same as basic italic.

THE LETTER t:

Please note that lowercase **t** is a short letter. Have older students compare height of **t**'s in different typefaces.

Getty-Dubay® Italic Handwriting Series – Letter Descriptions: Lowercase Family 7 & 8

OBJECTIVES: Halfway through first grade and thereafter, student knows stroke sequence of each letter and names of letter parts: *body height, downstroke, ascender, descender, crossbar, counter, elliptical curve* (as in *a, o*), and *arch*; after pp. 36 -37 in Book C, *entrance serif* and *exit serif, join* and *joining*. Student also understands the following terms from Book B on: *waistline, baseline, letter size, shape, stroke, slope* and *spacing*, and the concept of the imaginary *branching line*. In Books B and C student understands terms: *ascender line, descender line*.

EVALUATION: No one feels good about getting a workbook returned that is all marked with red. If one major difference from the model letter keeps recurring, make one note about it at top of student's page. In a color other than red, make a notation for you, then help that student later individually or in a small group.

BASIC

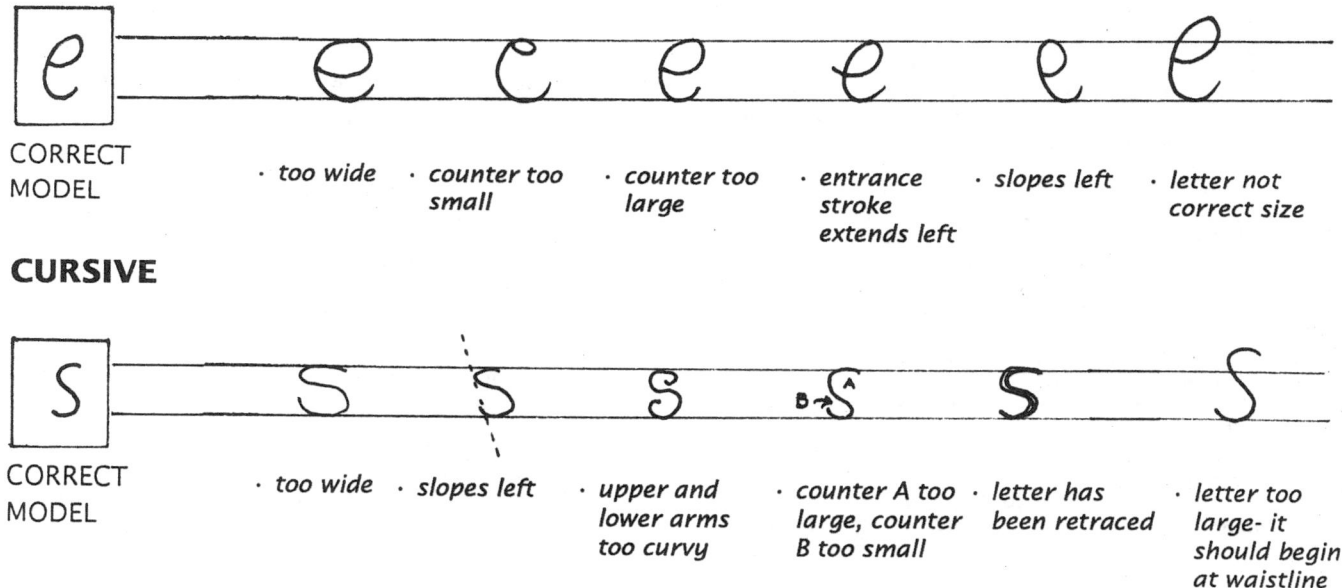

CORRECT MODEL

- too wide
- counter too small
- counter too large
- entrance stroke extends left
- slopes left
- letter not correct size

CURSIVE

CORRECT MODEL

- too wide
- slopes left
- upper and lower arms too curvy
- counter A too large, counter B too small
- letter has been retraced
- letter too large- it should begin at waistline

ACTIVITY: It's fun to write in cornmeal! Fill a roasting pan or 9" x13" pan to a depth of 1"-2". After every student has had a bit of time to explore the feeling of the cornmeal (probably over a period of several days), students take turns, one at a time, writing letters or words in the cornmeal with their forefingers. This helps the child who is having difficulty learning shape or correct sequence of strokes. Cornmeal is more expensive than sand, but it cleans up easily! It will last all year if you cover it TIGHTLY and put it away after each use. Use it for other activities too, but establish definite guidelines. (I always had cornmeal in my Kg, Gr. 1 & 2 rooms).

> A true secret of happiness
>   lies in taking a genuine interest
> in all the details of daily life,   WILLIAM MORRIS
>   in elevating them by art

GETTY-DUBAY® ITALIC HANDWRITING SERIES
BASIC ITALIC CAPITALS

All capitals begin at the capital height and sit on the baseline.

A Medium width
1st stroke: diagonal to baseline
2nd stroke: touching 1st stroke at top, diagonal to baseline
3rd stroke: horizontal from 1st stroke to 2nd stroke, slightly below center of capital height

B Narrow width
1st stroke: downstroke to baseline
2nd stroke: short horizontal from capital height into upper curve touching 1st stroke at center, lower curve to horizontal touching 1st stroke at baseline

C Wide width
wide curve to baseline ending slightly above baseline

D Wide width
1st stroke: downstroke to baseline
2nd stroke: short horizontal from capital height into wide curve to short horizontal at baseline touching 1st stroke

E Narrow width
1st stroke: downstroke to baseline, then horizontal
2nd stroke: horizontal at capital height
3rd stroke: horizontal beginning at center of 1st stroke

F Narrow width
1st stroke: downstroke to baseline
2nd stroke: horizontal at capital height
3rd stroke: horizontal beginning slightly below center of 1st stroke

G Wide width
1st stroke: wide curve to baseline
2nd stroke: horizontal at center of capital height, then downstroke touching 1st stroke near baseline (HINT: begin 2nd stroke in center of curve)

H Medium width
1st stroke: downstroke to baseline
2nd stroke: downstroke to baseline
3rd stroke: horizontal at center of capital height from 1st stroke to 2nd stroke

I Narrow width
1st stroke: downstroke to baseline
2nd stroke: short horizontal at capital height centered over 1st stroke
3rd stroke: short horizontal at baseline centered under 1st stroke

J Narrow width
downstroke into curve at baseline

K Medium width
1st stroke: downstroke to baseline
2nd stroke: diagonal from capital height touching 1st stroke at center, then diagonal to baseline

L Narrow width
downstroke to baseline, then horizontal on baseline

M Wide width
1st stroke: steep diagonal to baseline
2nd stroke: diagonal from top of 1st stroke to baseline, then diagonal up to capital height, then steep diagonal to baseline

N Medium width
1st stroke: downstroke to baseline
2nd stroke: diagonal from top of 1st stroke to baseline
3rd stroke: downstroke touching 2nd stroke at baseline

O Wide width
wide curve to baseline to wide curve overlapping beginning

P Narrow width
1st stroke: downstroke to baseline
2nd stroke: short horizontal from capital height into curve, ending slightly below center of downstroke

Q Wide width
1st stroke: wide curve to baseline to wide curve overlapping beginning
2nd stroke: diagonal from 1st stroke at baseline

R Narrow width
1st stroke: downstroke to baseline
2nd stroke: short horizontal from capital height into curve, to horizontal touching slightly below center of 1st stroke
3rd stroke: diagonal from 2nd stroke (slightly to the right of 1st stroke) to baseline

S Narrow width
horizontal into curve, to diagonal into curve, to horizontal

T Medium width
1st stroke: downstroke to baseline
2nd stroke: horizontal at capital height centered over 1st stroke

U Medium width
downstroke to curve at baseline into upstroke to capital height, then downstroke to baseline

V Medium width
diagonal to baseline, then diagonal to capital height

W Wide width
diagonal to baseline, then diagonal to capital height, then diagonal to baseline, then diagonal to capital height

X Medium width
1st stroke: diagonal to baseline
2nd stroke: diagonal from baseline to capital height crossing 1st stroke at center

Y Medium width
1st stroke: diagonal to center of capital height
2nd stroke: diagonal to center of capital height touching 1st stroke, then downstroke to baseline

Z Medium width
horizontal, then diagonal to baseline, then horizontal on baseline

GETTY-DUBAY® ITALIC HANDWRITING SERIES
CURSIVE ITALIC CAPITALS

All capitals begin at the capital height line with a downstroke, curve, sharp angle entrance serif, soft angle entrance serif, or curve entrance serif.

A 1st stroke: diagonal into curve exit serif at baseline
2nd stroke: touching 1st stroke at top, diagonal to baseline
3rd stroke: extended horizontal ending at 2nd stroke; position is slightly below center of capital height on the branching line.

B 1st stroke: downstroke to baseline
2nd stroke: curve entrance serif from waistline to capital height into upper curve of letter touching 1st stroke at center, lower curve of letter to horizontal touching 1st stroke at baseline

C wide curve to baseline ending slightly above baseline (same as basic)

D 1st stroke: downstroke to baseline
2nd stroke: curve entrance serif from waistline to capital height into wide curve of letter to horizontal touching 1st stroke at baseline

E 1st stroke: downstroke to baseline, horizontal
2nd stroke: curve entrance serif from waistline to capital height into horizontal
3rd stroke: horizontal beginning at center of 1st stroke

F 1st stroke: downstroke to baseline
2nd stroke: curve entrance serif from waistline to capital height into horizontal
3rd stroke: horizontal beginning slightly below center of 1st stroke

G wide curve to baseline to slightly below center of capital height, steep diagonal to baseline into curve exit serif at descender length

H 1st stroke: sharp angle entrance serif into downstroke into curve exit serif at baseline
2nd stroke: curve entrance serif beginning slightly higher than capital height into downstroke to baseline
3rd stroke: extended horizontal at center of capital height ending at 2nd stroke

I horizontal entrance serif into downstroke into horizontal exit serif at baseline

J horizontal entrance serif into downstroke into curve exit serif at descender length

K 1st stroke: sharp angle entrance serif into downstroke into curve exit serif at baseline
2nd stroke: diagonal from capital height touching 1st stroke at center, diagonal into curve exit serif at baseline

L curve entrance serif into downstroke to baseline, horizontal with short exit serif

M 1st stroke: steep diagonal to curve exit serif at baseline
2nd stroke: diagonal from top of 1st stroke to baseline, diagonal to capital height, steep diagonal to baseline

N 1st stroke: downstroke to curve exit serif at baseline
2nd stroke: diagonal from top of 1st stroke to baseline
3rd stroke: curve entrance serif beginning slightly higher than capital height into downstroke touching 2nd stroke at baseline

O wide curve to baseline to wide curve to overlap beginning (same as basic)

P 1st stroke: downstroke to baseline
2nd stroke: curve entrance serif from waist line to capital height into curve of letter ending at 1st stroke slightly below center

Q 1st stroke: wide curve to baseline to wide curve to overlap beginning
2nd stroke: diagonal from 1st stroke at baseline (slightly to the right of center) into short exit serif at the descender length (same as basic)

R 1st stroke: downstroke to baseline
2nd stroke: curve entrance serif from waistline to capital height into curve of letter to horizontal touching 1st stroke slightly below center
3rd stroke: diagonal from 2nd stroke (slightly to the right of 1st stroke) into curve exit serif at baseline

S horizontal to curve to diagonal to curve to horizontal (same as basic)

T 1st stroke: downstroke to baseline.
2nd stroke: curve entrance serif from waistline to capital height into horizontal

U soft angle entrance serif into downstroke to curve at baseline to upstroke to capital height, downstroke to baseline

V curve entrance serif into diagonal to baseline, diagonal to capital height

W curve entrance serif into diagonal to baseline, diagonal to capital height, diagonal to baseline, diagonal to capital height

X 1st stroke: curve entrance serif into diagonal into curve exit serif
2nd stroke: diagonal from baseline to capital height crossing 1st stroke at center

Y soft angle entrance serif into downstroke to curve at baseline to upstroke to capital height, downstroke to baseline into curve exit serif descender length. (The only basic capital that changes in cursive.)

Z short entrance serif into horizontal, diagonal to baseline, horizontal into short exit serif

GETTY-DUBAY® ITALIC HANDWRITING SERIES
NUMERALS

The word NUMBER stands for an idea - how many objects in a certain group.
The word NUMERAL describes the symbol we use for the number idea.

Just as the first writing happened long after people began speaking, writing numerals to represent numbers came long after people began counting. The earliest numerals known were marks on stones and notices in sticks.

About 3,400 BCE, the Egyptians developed a written number system using hieroglyphics, as shown:

I stroke ~ 1	II	III	IIII	III II	III III	IIII III	IIII IIII	III III III	⌒ arch ~ 10
1⌒	II⌒	⌒⌒	⌒⌒⌒	⌒⌒⌒⌒	ⓖ coiled rope ~ 100		ⓖⓖ ⌒⌒⌒ IIII How would we write this? ____		

One problem with the Egyptian system and those of the Greeks and the Romans is that none of them had a symbol to represent zero, "Not any." In most early systems, people formed numerals by repeating a few basic symbols, then adding their values.

The numerals we use most likely came by way of Arabia from a starting point in India. The Indians had a superior system — a base of ten and symbols for each number from one to nine. This was about 300 BCE. The use of the numeral zero we know today probably first took hold in India in the 5th century CE. Later, these numerals arrived in Europe, by way of Spain, and were developed into the system we use and that is used in most parts of the world today.

Beginning of our numerals

O	—	=	≡	W+E (N/S compass)	✋	✶✶✶ ✶✶✶✶ possibly from 7 stars in Big Dipper constellation	beginnings of 6, 8, & 9 unknown
meaning no-thing							

HINDU-ARABIC NUMERALS
Use large numerals when writing with all large caps.

0 0 1 1 2 2 3 3 4 4 5 5 6 6 7 7 8 8 9 9
                             or 4   or 7

Use small numerals with lowercase and caps and for math.

0 1 2 3 4 5 6 7 8 9
        or 4

Hindu – Arabic Numerals

ROMAN NUMERALS

I	II	III	IV	V	VI	VII	VIII	IX	X	XI	XII
			5-1=4	5	5+1=6			10-1=9	10	10+1=11	

Roman Numerals are written vertically with no slope.

XX	L	C	D	M	·	MCMLXXXVIII
10+10=20	50	100	500	1,000		1000+(1000-100)+50+10+10+10+5+1+1+1=1988

Money amounts and metric system abbreviations

$15.27   98¢   6 cm   124 kg   539 km
                          centimeters   kilograms   kilometers

Time and temperature

8:30 a.m.   12:45 p.m.   74°F   30°C
ante meridian–before noon   post meridian–after noon   Fahrenheit   Celsius

Phone number, abbreviated date, height or length

(123) 456-7890   3/20/94   5'7"   8¾
area code prefix number   asterisk   fraction

Punctuation and other symbols

. , ' ? ! " " — – ( ) ¢ $ $1^{x^2}_{etc.}$ / & &
apostrophe   hyphen dash parentheses   slant or slash ampersands

GETTY-DUBAY® ITALIC HANDWRITING SERIES
TRANSITION FROM BASIC ITALIC TO CURSIVE ITALIC

ADDITIONS & OPTIONS:

OPTION: f adds a descender

f · f

OPTION: i and j use a dot or jot

i · i or i   j · j or j

OPTION: k may also be a one-stroke letter

k · k or k

SERIFS: Serifs are lines added to letters. There are exit serifs and entrance serifs.

Serifs are like hands reaching out to join letters.

EXIT SERIF: End with a soft angle at the baseline into a short diagonal. (n, m, and x also have entrance serifs.)

a · a · a   d · d · d   h · h · h   i · i · i

k · k · k   l · l · l   m · m · m   n · n · n

u · u · u   x · x · x   AVOID a hook   AVOID a scoop

ENTRANCE SERIFS: There are two kinds of entrance serifs—soft angle entrance serifs and sharp angle entrance serifs.

SOFT ANGLE ENTRANCE SERIF: Begin with a short diagonal line to a soft angle.

(m, n, and x have exit serifs also)

m · m · m   n · n · n   r · r · r   x · x · x

SHARP ANGLE ENTRANCE SERIF: Begin with a short diagonal line to a sharp angle.

AVOID a scoop

j · j · j   p · p · p   v · v · v   w · w · w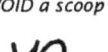

CURSIVE Z: Add short entrance and exit serifs to z.   z · z · z

LETTERS THAT REMAIN THE SAME: b c e g o q s t y

GETTY-DUBAY® ITALIC HANDWRITING SERIES
CURSIVE ITALIC JOIN DESCRIPTIONS

JOIN 1: DIAGONAL

an Join from the baseline into n, m, r, and x.
Join out of a, c, d, e, h, i, k, l, m, n, u, and z.

 1. straight diagonal line from baseline to waistline

 2. soft angle entrance serif into n, m, r, and x

AVOID a wavy line

añ añ ar ax · an cn dn en
hn in kn or kn ln mn nn un zn

OPTION: Diagonal swing up into n, m, r, and x. (See JOIN 2 below.)

JOIN 2: DIAGONAL SWING UP

au Join from the baseline into u, y, i, j, p, t, l, h, b, k, v, and w.
Join out of a, c, d, e, h, i, k, l, m, n, u, and z.
OPTION: Join from the baseline into n, m, r, and x.

 1. straight diagonal line from baseline to branching line

 2. swing up from branching line to waistline into u, y, i, j, p, t, l, h, b, k, v, and w.

AVOID scoop and loop

au ay ai aj ap at al ah ab ak or ak
av aw · au cu du eu hu iu ku or ku
lu mu nu uu zu

OPTION: Diagonal swing up into n, m, r, and x.

an am ar ax

Getty-Dubay® Italic Handwriting Series - Cursive Italic Join Descriptions

JOIN 3: DIAGONAL START BACK

ao Join from the baseline into o and optional join into s.
Join out of a, c, d, e, h, i, k, l, m, n, u, and z.

1. straight diagonal line from baseline to waistline
2. start back down 1/3 of the diagonal into o and s 

AVOID wave

OPTION: ao as · ao co do eo ho io ko or ko lo mo no uo zo

OPTION: Join into **s** from the baseline to the waistline, leaving off the horizontal top of s.   es is us

OPTION: See Join 8 where the **s** shape is unchanged.   es is us

JOIN 4: DIAGONAL INTO e

ae Join from the baseline into e at the branching line.
Join out of a, c, d, e, h, i, k, l, m, n, u, and z.

1. straight diagonal line from baseline to branching line
2. begin e at the branching line 

AVOID scoop

ae · ae ce de ee he ie ke or ke le me ne ue ze

OPTION: Lift before **e** from baseline.   ae ee ie ue

OPTION: Two-stroke e
  Join into e with a straight, diagonal line from the baseline to the waistline, then start back down into e (Join 3).
  Join out of the center of e with a diagonal, following back out of the second stroke with a diagonal to the waistline.

e ae en   ueu mem nen

Getty-Dubay® Italic Handwriting Series - Cursive Italic Join Descriptions

JOIN 5: HORIZONTAL

on Join with a horizontal out of o, t, f, v, w, and x.
Join into all letters except f. (Optional into z.)

on 1. straight horizontal line at the waistline

oe diagonal into e out of o, v, w, and x.

AVOID scoop *ou*

on tn fn vn wn xn · oa ob oc od
og oh oi oj ok or ok ol om on op oq
or os ot ou ov ow ox oy oz

OPTION: Join into **e** from waistline.   oe ve we xe te fe

OPTION: Lift before **e** from waistline.   oe ve we xe te fe

OPTION: Join into **e** out of the first stroke of **t**.   te

JOIN 6: DIAGONAL OUT OF r

rn Join with a short diagonal out of r into all letters except f.

rn 1. diagonal out of r to waistline

re diagonal out of r to center of e (slightly above branching line)

AVOID rn looking like m   *rn*

rn · ra rb rc rd re rg rh ri rj rk or rk
rl rm rn ro rp rq rr rs rt ru
rv rw rx ry rz

OPTION: Lift after **r**.

rn · ra rb rc rd re rg rh ri rj rk or rk
rl rm rn ro rp rq rr rs rt ru
rv rw rx ry rz

NOTE: When lifting between letters, be sure to keep letters close together.
Joins are natural spacers — when not using a join, keep letters close.

Getty-Dubay® Italic Handwriting Series - Cursive Italic Join Descriptions

JOIN 7: HORIZONTAL TO DIAGONAL

su

Join from the baseline out of s, b, and p.
Join into all letters except f and z.

su   1. horizontal at the baseline   *su so*   2. blend into a diagonal to either the branching line or the waistline

AVOID scoop *su*

sb se sh si sj sk or sk sl sm sn so sp sr
ss st su sv sw sx sy · be pe br pr

OPTION: Lift after **s**, **b**, and **p**.   su ss bu bb pu pp se be pe

JOIN 8: DIAGONAL TO HORIZONTAL

aa

Join from the baseline into a, c, d, g, q, and s.
Join out of a, b, c, d, e, h, i, k, l, m, n, p, s, u, and z.

aa   1. diagonal from the baseline to the waistline   *aa*   2. horizontal at the waistline

AVOID wave *aa*

aa ac ad ag aq as
aa ba ca da ea ha ia ka or ka la
ma na pa sa ua za

OPTION: Lift before **a**, **c**, **d**, **g**, **q**, and **s** when joining from the baseline.

aa ac ad ag aq as

LIFTS: Lift before f and z. (Optional join into z from waistline.)
Lift after g, j, q, and y.

AVOID gap *af*

af az gu ju qu yu

NOTE: When lifting between letters, be sure to keep letters close together.
Joins are natural spacers — when not using a join, keep letters close..

READING LOOPED CURSIVE

There are both similarities and differences between looped cursive and italic cursive. There are six major and two minor lowercase letter shape differences. The other eighteen letters remain the same except for the formation of ascenders and descenders on eight letters. If looped cursive is written legibly it is not difficult to read. It is poorly written looped cursive that presents most recognition problems.

Ways Parents and Teachers Can Help Students Read Looped Cursive

1. Review page 51, *"Comparing Cursive Italic to Looped Cursive."*

2. It is suggested from mid-third grade on that the teacher spend five minutes per week teaching recognition of looped cursive. Students do not need to write the letters but do need to build decoding skills.

3. Write a looped cursive letter and have the students identify it (but not write it). Start with lower-case, one letter at a time. Compare it with the italic form. Begin with letters underlined with dots, then letters with lines.

   Write simple words using letters already introduced. Ask the students to read the word.

   Finally, progress to sentence reading of looped cursive.

4. Have students read looped cursive handwriting samples.

5. Collect incoming mail envelopes to the same address (any handwriting style). Compare with regard to ease of reading. Note which ones are carefully written and those which are poorly written and more difficult to read. Point to specific problems in decoding.

.... resembles italic form, but may be difficult for student to identify

_____ little or no resemblance to the italic form

READING LOOPED CURSIVE
COMPARING GETTY-DUBAY® CURSIVE ITALIC WITH LOOPED CURSIVE

Look at the examples of cursive italic and looped cursive. Compare the two styles of writing. Notice the differences in letter shape, letter slope, capital height, ascender height, and descender length.

There are many styles of writing you need to be able to read. Practice reading looped cursive. To help read the looped cursive letters, each name contains both a capital letter and its lowercase version.

SHAPE:
Look at the different shapes of the looped cursive lowercase letters b, f, r, s, and z and the capital letters F, G, I, J, Q, S, T, V, X, and Z.

SLOPE:
Look at the slope difference. Cursive Italic letter slope is 5° and looped cursive is 30°.

SIZE:
Look at the size difference. Cursive italic capitals, ascenders, and descenders are 1 1/2 body heights. Looped cursive capitals, ascenders and descenders are 2 body heights.

Compare the absence of loops in cursive italic with the many loops in looped cursive. Look at how the capitals, ascenders, and descenders become tangled in the looped cursive.
Loop-free italic is easier to read.

5° slope   30° slope

Angela / Angela
Barbara / Barbara
Cecilia / Cecilia
David / David
Eugene / Eugene
Fifi / Fifi
Gregory / Gregory
Hannah / Hannah
Irving / Irving
Jojo / Jojo
Kirk / Kirk
Lillian / Lillian
Malcolm / Malcolm
Nancy / Nancy
Otto / Otto
Philippa / Philippa
Queequeg / Queequeg
Richard / Richard
Susan / Susan
Trent / Trent
Ursula / Ursula
Vivian / Vivian
Woodrow / Woodrow
Xerxes / Xerxes
Yonny / Yonny
Zanzi / Zanzi

GETTY-DUBAY® ITALIC HANDWRITING SERIES
SEQUENCE OF SKILLS

Program Goal
To write neat, legible handwriting without prompts as a scaffold to English Language Literacy

The Student	K (25-50 min/wk)	1 (30-100 min/wk)	2 (45-100 min/wk)	3 (60-120 min/wk)	4 (60-120 min/wk)	5 (60-120 min/wk)	6 (40 min/wk)
holds and uses writing tool correctly	■	■	■	■	■	■	■
sits correctly	■	■	■	■	■	■	■
positions the paper correctly	■	■	■	■	■	■	■
writes letters in a top-to-bottom progression (except d and e)	■	■	■	■	■	■	■
writes all lowercase letters (8 family groups)	■	■	■	■	■	■	■
writes his/her name in basic italic	■	■	■	■	■	■	■
writes numerals	■	■	■	■	■	■	■
writes words and sentences in basic italic	■	■	■	■	■	■	■
writes with a consistent letter slope		■	■	■	■	■	■
evaluates his/her own handwriting according to letter shapes, slope, and strokes		■	■	■	■	■	■
uses correct spacing within words and between words to develop legible handwriting		■	■	■	■	■	■
writes words, sentences and paragraphs in basic italic			■	■	■	■	■
uses margins and headings appropriately			■	■	■	■	■
writes the cursive italic joins 1-5			■	■	■	■	■
continues to use basic italic for maps, charts, posters, forms, etc.				■	■	■	■
reads looped cursive				■	■	■	■
writes cursive italic joins 1-8				■	■	■	■
writes cursive italic capitals				■	■	■	■
writes his/her name in cursive italic				■	■	■	■
is able to make various join option choices				■	■	■	■
can discern among various historical scripts							■
experiences writing with an edged pen							■

Getty-Dubay® Italic Handwriting Assessment

Letter Dimensions
Assessment Questions
Assessment Chart
Assessment in the Elementary Classroom

·abcdefghijklmnopqrstuvwxyz·

GETTY-DUBAY® ITALIC HANDWRITING SERIES
ASSESSMENT

For the student:

1 LOOK: Personal Best

LOOK at your writing.
Pick your best letter.
Answer the question.

LOOK at your writing.
Pick your best join.
Answer the question.

✎ *Circle your best...*
✎ *Are you writing...*

For the teacher:
LOOK: Personal Best

Direct the student to *LOOK* carefully at his/her writing. Look at one letter dimension at a time — shape, size, slope, or spacing. Use the italic handwriting vocabulary (page 15) to describe the specific letter dimensions. Direct the student to pick and circle his/her best letter or join. It may not be perfect, but it is the best one at the moment. This is the student's personal best. Assessment is built on a positive note based on success.

Direct the student to answer the question. A 'Yes' answer means OK, task accomplished; a 'No' answer means work to be done. All the Yes/No answers in the books are near the right hand margin of each page for easy access by the teacher. Assessment questions are found in the workbooks and the INSTRUCTION MANUAL. They may be supplemented by the teacher and student. Some of the questions refer to the process of writing, such as pencil hold, stroke direction, stroke sequence. Most of the questions refer to letter dimensions.

See Assessment Questions:
basic lowercase, pages 62-63
basic capitals, page 64
cursive lowercase joins, page 66
cursive capitals, page 65

REMINDER: The student may need help with the process of writing. As needed, remind the student of the correct pencil hold, paper position, posture, stroke direction, and stroke sequence.

For the student:

2 PLAN: Prescription for success

PLAN which letters
need work. How will
you make them look
more like the models?

Pick the joins that need
work. Compare them
with the models.
PLAN how to make the
joins look more like
the models.

For the teacher:
PLAN: Prescription for success

Assist the student to *PLAN* which letters need work and how to make them look more like the models. Direct the student to compare his/her writing with the models. Ask, *"How is your letter different from the model?"*, rather than saying it is wrong. Use the italic handwriting vocabulary to describe how the letter should look. First consider letter shape, then size, slope, then spacing. As you begin the assessment focus on (1) what is going well, then describe (2) what needs to be improved, and then prescribe (3) what to do to make the improvement.

For example:

SHAPE: (1) The downstroke of **n** is nice and straight.
n (2) The **n** is branching higher than halfway.
n (3) Branch out at the branching line.

SIZE: (1) The **n** sits perfectly on the baseline.
n (2) The arch of **n** is higher than the body height.
n (3) Make the arch of **n** touch the waistline.

SLOPE: (1) The slope of **a** and **d** in 'and' looks nice and even.
and (2) The **n** is sloping more than the other letters in the word.
and (3) Use the same slope for all the letters.

SPACING: (1) The spacing between **n** and **d** in 'and' looks good–it's just close enough.
and (2) There is more space between **a** and **n** than between **n** and **d**.
and (3) Make the space between **a** and **n** equal to the space between **n** and **d**.

See Letter Descriptions, pages 32-43
See Cursive Join Descriptions, pages 46-49

For the student:

 PRACTICE: Improvement

>PRACTICE the letters that need more work.
>
>PRACTICE the joins that need more work.
>
>PRACTICE on lined paper. Use paper with a capital line if needed. (See INSTRUCTION MANUAL)

For the teacher:
PRACTICE: Improvement

Allow time for the student to PRACTICE the letters or joins that need work. Follow the PLAN. Provide lined paper for the student to use for practicing after writing in the workbook. The student may need to do more tracing of the letters in order to kinesthetically learn the shapes. Place tracing paper or any thin paper over the models and trace the letters as needed.

Practicing on the board is helpful for the student who need to refine large muscle coordination. Using an overhead, project lines for the student to write on the chalkboard. Letters may be projected onto the chalkboard for the student to trace.

Encourage the student to assess the practice. When improvement is made, the student may write a star at the top of his/her page. Ask the student to tell how the writing has improved.

OPTIONS: Each person has an individual style of writing, just as each person is unique. Encourage each student to write the best he/she can and to find the most comfortable writing style. Options in shape include standard, compressed, and expanded. Options in size include any body height that can be read easily. Options in slope are between a vertical of 0° and a slope of 15°. Options in spacing include standard, compressed and expanded. Whichever combinations of options are chosen, the goal is consistent, even, legible handwriting. See *Options* page 56.

RECORDS: Records of the student's progress are rewarding and useful. A simple plus, check, and minus code, referring to specific letter dimensions, may be used for recording student progress. A plus indicates "well done", a check indicates one or two improvements need to be made, and a minus indicates a number of improvements need to be made. As improvements are made the minus or check can be turned into a plus. Dates on the record indicate the rate of progress.

Have the student place examples of his/her best handwriting in his/her own Student Portfolio. The examples may be the teacher's choice or the student's choice.

Direct the student to do the Pre-test at the beginning of each workbook and the Post-test after completing each workbook.

ASSESSMENT BY TEACHER, TEACHER/STUDENT, AND STUDENT

At the beginning of the year, the teacher models the assessment process by reviewing student work and using specific letter dimensions. Next, the teacher and student jointly assess the progress and plan for further success. Finally, the student independently analyzes, prescribes, and self-corrects his/her efforts toward the goal.

GETTY-DUBAY® ITALIC HANDWRITING SERIES
OPTIONS

A personal handwriting style is created by variations of shape, size, slope, spacing, and speed.

SHAPE
Italic is based on an elliptical shape which may be standard, expanded, or compressed. See *Shape Guidelines*, page 57.

Standard — a quick brown fox jumps over the lazy dog

Expanded — a quick brown fox jumps over the

Compressed — a quick brown fox jumps over the lazy dog

SIZE
Each person has a comfortable letter size. See *Size Guidelines*, page 58.

4mm   3mm   2½mm

a quick brown fox jumps over the lazy dog

SLOPE
Writing slope may vary from 0° to 15°. Standard slope is 5°. Whichever slope is preferred, be consistent. See *Slope Guidelines*, page 59.

0° — a quick brown fox jumps over the lazy dog

5° (standard) — a quick brown fox jumps over the lazy dog

10° — a quick brown fox jumps over the lazy dog

15° — a quick brown fox jumps over the lazy dog

SPACING
The spacing between letters in a word and between words may be standard, expanded, or compressed. See *Spacing Guidelines*, page 60.

Standard spacing — a quick brown fox jumps over the lazy dog

Expanded spacing — a quick brown fox jumps over the

Compressed spacing — a quick brown fox jumps over the lazy dog

SPEED
Let the speed of writing fit the need, maintaining legibility. Notice how speed affects shape, size, slope, and spacing. See *Speed Guidelines*, pages 60–61.

Moderate speed — a quick brown fox jumps over the lazy dog

Rapid speed — a quick brown fox jumps over the lazy

As you progress, italic handwriting becomes personal and unique. Whichever combinations of options are used, the goal is even shape, even size, even slope, and even spacing.

Getty-Dubay® Italic Handwriting Series - Assessment Guidelines

LETTER DIMENSIONS: SHAPE GUIDELINES

BASIC LOWERCASE: Basic italic lowercase has eight families grouped according to similarity of shape.

Family 1: straight line downstroke i j l
Family 2: diagonal k v w x z
Family 3: arch n h m r
Family 4: inverted arch u y
Family 5: basic a shape a d g q
Family 6: inverted basic a shape b p
Family 7: elliptical curve o e c s
Family 8: crossbar f t

The basic lowercase letters are written with one continuous stroke, except the crossed letters **f**, **t**, and **x**, the dotted letters **i** and **j**, and **k**. All letters are the same width as **o**, except **i**, **l**, and **r** are narrower and **m** and **w** are wider. Lowercase letters are presented first, since we read and write lowercase approximately 98% of the time.

CURSIVE LOWERCASE: The same letter shapes and slope are used for basic italic and cursive italic. The transition from basic italic to cursive italic is a natural one, building on previously learned concepts. Entrance and exit serifs are added to basic lowercase for cursive. There are eight join types; seven using diagonal connections and one using a horizontal connection.

an an an an
basic italic / serifs added / serifs joined / cursive italic

CAPITALS: Basic capitals are divided into three width groups.

    Wide: C G O Q D M W
   Medium: T H A N K U V X Y Z
   Narrow: E F L B P R S J I

Cursive capitals retain the same shape as basic italic with the addition of serifs. Only **Y** changes shape.
OPTION: A student may prefer to use basic capitals with cursive lowercase.

OPTIONS: The lowercase letters are modeled after the standard shape. Expanded and compressed letter shapes are acceptable as individual options. Whichever choice is made, the goal is to be consistent.

STANDARD Width is slightly more than half the body height

EXPANDED Width is slightly less than the body height.

COMPRESSED Width is close to half the body height.

See *Options*, page 56.

ASSESSMENT: Use this assessment process with your students.
LOOK at your writing. Do your letters look like the models?
Using 3-ring notebook paper, place one of the holes over a letter to single out that letter. For example: Are the **o**'s similar in width? Compare the width of **o** to an **n** or another letter of the same width.

See *Assessment Questions*:
   Basic italic lowercase, page 62–63
   Basic italic capitals, page 64
   Cursive italic capitals, page 65

PLAN how to make the letters look more like the models.
See *Letter Descriptions*:
   Basic & cursive italic lowercase, pages 32–41
   Basic italic capitals, page 42
   Cursive italic capitals, page 43

LETTER DIMENSIONS: SIZE GUIDELINES

All letters sit on the baseline, except **j** and cursive **f**. The waistline indicates the top of the body height—the height of an **x** or any letter without an ascender or descender. The size of capitals and letters with ascenders or descenders is $1\frac{1}{2}$ times the body height. The cursive **f**, having both an ascender and descender, is 2 times the body height. This size relationship allows lines of writing close together without tangling capitals and ascenders with descenders.

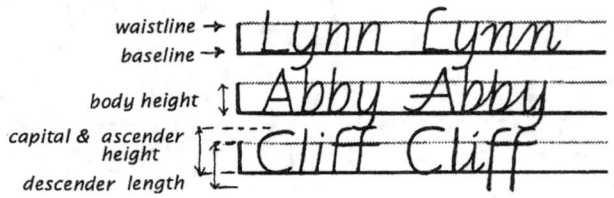

This size relationship is similar to many typefaces used in books and on computers.

The body heights used in the *Getty-Dubay® Italic Handwriting Series* are:

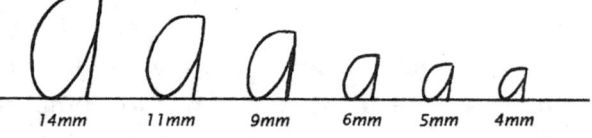

OPTIONS: Each person has a comfortable size of writing. When the young student begins to write, he/she should write without lines, thereby choosing letter height. When writing on lined paper, let the student choose his/her own letter height. Whatever letter height is chosen, the goal is to maintain a consistent size.

See *Options*, page 56.

ASSESSMENT: Use this assessment process with your students.

LOOK at your writing. Are you writing with an even letter size?
To check for even body height, draw a line parallel to the baseline touching the top of the body height of most of the letters. A slight variation is acceptable. If the variation is too great, the writing has an uneven look.

If the body height is too small, it is too difficult to read and the student must change to a size that is legible. Encourage the student to adjust his/her writing size to different sized spaces.

PLAN how to write with an even letter size.
Use a waistline as well as a baseline if needed; see *Size Guide* below. Use lines with a capital height line if needed (see lines on pages 102-108). As the student progresses, the goal is even size writing using only a baseline. The letter height size is the student's personal choice.

SIZE GUIDE: To maintain a consistent body height, a size guide is helpful. Take two sheets of notebook paper (see sizes below) and shift one sheet down half a space (or less than half a space). The faint line showing through will serve as a waistline. Fasten the two sheets with paper clips. It may be helpful to trace the lines on the second sheet with a ballpoint or fiber-tip pen in order to see the lines more easily.

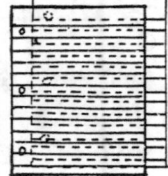

NOTEBOOK PAPER SIZES (actual sizes may vary)

9mm space / 4½ mm body height — notebook paper wide ruled

7mm space / 3¾ mm body height — notebook paper college ruled

LETTER DIMENSIONS: SLOPE GUIDELINES

A natural slope for handwriting is slightly slanted to the right from the vertical. The *Getty-Dubay® Italic Handwriting Series* is written with a 5° slope. Basic italic and cursive italic are written with the same 5° slope; there is no need to change slope.

The *Getty-Dubay® Italic Handwriting Series* offers a choice of slope—from a vertical of 0° to a slope of 15°. *Slope Guidelines* are shown in BOOKS D, E, F, and G offering a slope choice. Whichever slope is preferred, the goal is to maintain a consistent slope. The choice range is:

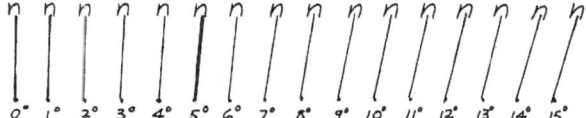

NOTE: As we write we all vary slightly from our chosen slope. We are not machines! An overall, even, balanced writing is our goal.
See *Options*, page 56.

SLOPE ASSESSMENT EXERCISE: Use this assessment process exercise with your students.
LOOK at your writing. Are you writing with an even slope? Are you using a 5° slope? What is your choice of slope?
If the slope is uneven, use the following exercise to find the student's natural slope:

1. Student writes a word.
2. Check the consistency of the slope by drawing slope lines through the center of each letter (line up with the downstroke or axis of each letter).
3. Choose the slope which appears most often, as in Example A or choose the slope in the middle range, as in Example B.
4. Then draw parallel lines next to the slope you have chosen.
5. Use the parallel lines as your slope guide.

	EXAMPLE A	EXAMPLE B
1. Write word.		
2. Draw slope lines over letters		
3. Pick one slope		
4. Draw parallel lines		
5. Write over slope lines		

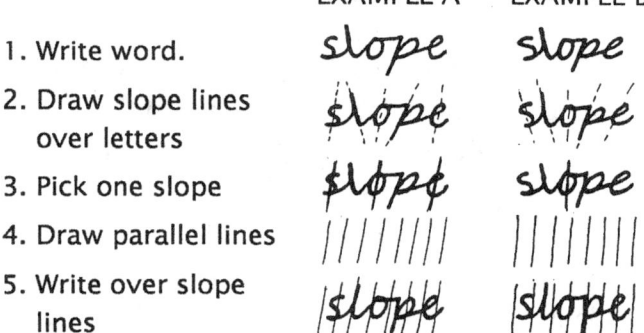

PLAN how to write with an even slope.
Use a slope guide under the writing paper. For a guide to fit a personal choice of slope, see *Slope Guide* below. If the slope is more than 15° or a backhand is used, changing the paper position often helps. (Generally, a backhand slope is difficult to read; a slight backhand slope is acceptable.)
As the student progresses, the goal is to write with a consistent slope of the student's choice (between 0° and 15°).

SLOPE GUIDE: To maintain a consistent letter slope a slope guide is helpful. Use a sheet of notebook paper positioned at an angle underneath the writing paper so that the lines line up with the student's chosen slope. Use paper clips to hold in place. Outline the edge of the writing paper on the slope guide so it can be easily repositioned under other lined paper. The student writes his/her name on the individualized slope guide.

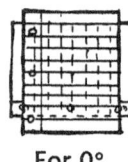
For 0°

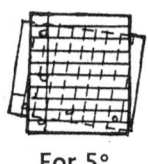
For 5°

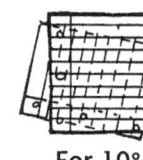
For 10°

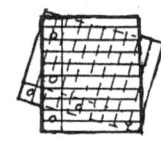
For 15°

LETTER DIMENSIONS: SPACING GUIDELINES

There are two aspects of spacing: the space between letters within a word and the space between words in a sentence.

Space between letters:
The letters within a word are close together. In basic italic, there are three rules of spacing:

 1. Two downstrokes are the farthest apart.

 2. A downstroke and a curve are a little closer.

3. Two curves are the closest; almost touching.

In cursive italic, joins are natural spacers. When lifts occur between letters (before **f** and **z**; after **g**, **j**, **q**, and **y**), keep letters close together to avoid gaps.

Space between words:
BOOKS A and B: Leave the width of the young student's two fingers between words. BOOK C and beginning of BOOK D: Leave the width of **m** between words. BOOKS D, E, F, and G: Leave the width of **n** between words.
OPTIONS: Standard spacing is used in the *Italic Handwriting Series*. Expanded and compressed spacing are other choices.
See *Options*, page 56.
ASSESSMENT: Use this assessment process with your students.
LOOK at your writing. Are your letters spaced evenly in words? Are you using the correct width between words?
Whichever spacing is used, the goal is to maintain consistent, even spacing.
PLAN how to write with even spacing.
Compare writing with the models. If there is a gap between letters in a word, place letters closer together. If a student writes with more compressed or expanded spacing, aim for consistency. Depending on student level, use the width of two fingers, **m**, or **n** to check the correct space between words.

LETTER DIMENSIONS: SPEED GUIDELINES

Writing speed is highly individual. Each person has a comfortable speed of writing. Let the speed fit the need. Speed is not a primary concern in BOOKS A, B, and C. After all the joins are learned, begin to increase speed using the *Timed Writing* exercise (see next page and BOOKS D, E, F, and G). Repeat exercise at least once a month.

OPTIONS: There are three general speeds of writing:
1. slow speed for learning letter shapes and for formal writing
2. moderate speed for everyday informal writing
3. fast speed for note taking and other rapid writing

Whichever speed is used, the goal is to write legibly.
See *Options*, page 56.

ASSESSMENT: Use this assessment process with your students.
LOOK at your writing. Is your writing speed allowing you to write legibly? Can you read your writing? Can other people read your writing? Does your writing speed fit the writing need?
Speed can be increased without decreasing legibility. This is done gradually, so there is minimal pressure or stress involved. Use the *Timed Writing* exercise on the following page or in BOOKS D, E, F, and G. Follow up with *Eyes Closed* writing exercise (not timed). Students enjoy this exercise and are often amazed to see how well they can write with their eyes closed. It is a great confidence builder.
PLAN how to fit the speed to the need.
Write slower if the letter shapes, size, slope or spacing need more attention. Write a little faster if the writing task requires it, maintaining legibility. Adjust the writing speed to fit the need.

Getty-Dubay® Italic Handwriting Series - Assessment: Speed

> **TIMED WRITING** Use the timed writing to help increase speed for formal, informal, & rapid writing.

Begin by writing the following sentence on another sheet of paper as a warm-up for the timed writing. If you prefer, substitute another pangram or sentence.

A quick brown fox jumps over the lazy dog.

1. TIME LENGTH: 1 MINUTE Write the sentence at your most comfortable speed. If you finish before the time is up, begin the sentence again.

_____

_____

Count the number of words written and write the number in Box 1.   [ ] Box 1

2. TIME LENGTH: 1 MINUTE Write the sentence a little faster. Try to add 1 or 2 more words to your total.

_____

_____

Write the number of words written in Box 2.   [ ] Box 2

3. TIME LENGTH: 1 MINUTE Write the sentence as fast as you can. Maintain legibility.

_____

_____

Write the number of words written in Box 3.   [ ] Box 3

4. TIME LENGTH: 1 MINUTE Write the sentence at a comfortable speed.

_____

_____

Write number of words written in Box 4.   [ ] Box 4

The goal is to increase the number of words written per minute. Aim for an increase in the total of Box 4 over Box 1. Speed can be increased while maintaining legibility. Repeat process once a month.

EYES CLOSED Using the same sentence, do this exercise as a follow-up to timed writing. Begin with a non-lined sheet of paper. Close your eyes. Picture in your mind's eye the shape of each letter as you write. Take all the time you need. You may be amazed how well you can write with your eyes closed.

For inservice instruction, this page may be copied as projection transparency and/or teacher handout.

© 2012 Getty-Dubay
Getty-Dubay™ Italic Handwriting Series
available at www.handwritingsuccess.com

GETTY-DUBAY® ITALIC HANDWRITING SERIES
ASSESSMENT QUESTIONS: BASIC ITALIC LOWERCASE

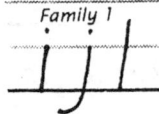

FAMILY 1: STRAIGHT LINE DOWNSTROKE i j l
    Are you starting at the large dot and following the arrow? (BOOKS A,B,C)
    Do your first strokes start at the top?
    Are your downstrokes of i and l straight lines?
    Does your i start at the waistline?
    Does your l start at the ascender height?
    Does your j start at the waistline?
    Does your j end at the descender length?
    Do your i and l sit on the baseline?
    Is your descender of j a curve ending with a short horizontal?
    Are the dots of i and j directly over the downstrokes?
    Do your letters look like the models?

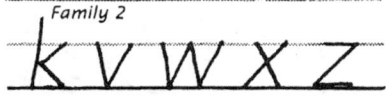

FAMILY 2: DIAGONAL k v w x z
    Are you starting at the large dot and following the arrow? (BOOKS A,B,C)
    Do your letters start at the top?
    Do your letters sit on the baseline?
    Are your diagonals straight lines?
    Do your v and w begin and end at the waistline?
    Is your w wider than k, v, x, and z?
    Are your two v shapes in w each narrower than a single v?
    Do all the lines in your w touch the waistline?
    Does your second stroke of x start at the baseline?
    Do the two diagonals of your x cross at the branching line?
    Does your k begin at the ascender height?
    Does your second stroke of k touch the first stroke at the branching line?
    Does the second stroke of your k form a right angle (like the corner of a sheet of paper)?
    Does your z begin and end with a horizontal?
    Do your letters look like the models?

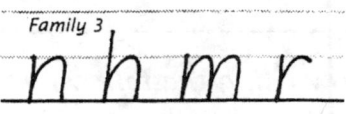

FAMILY 3: ARCH n m h r
    Are you starting at the large dot and following the arrow? (BOOKS A,B,C)
    Do your letters start at the top?
    Are you beginning all your letters with a straight line downstroke?
    Do your letters sit on the baseline?
    Are your letters branching at the branching line?
    Are you branching at the branching line to make the arch?
    Are the two sides of the arch parallel?
    Does the curve of your arch begin and end at the branching line?
    Does the curve of your arch touch the waistline?
    Are your h and n the same width?
    Is your m wider than n?
    Are your two arch shapes in m each narrower than a single arch of n?
    Do your m, n, and r begin at the waistline?
    Does your h begin at the ascender line?
    Is your r slightly narrower than n?
    Does your arm of r bend down after touching the waistline?
    Do your letters look like the models?

FAMILY 4: INVERTED (UPSIDE-DOWN) ARCH u y
    Are you starting at the large dot and following the arrow? (BOOKS A,B,C)
    Do your letters start at the top?
    Does your u sit on the baseline?
    Does your y end at the descender length?
    Is your descender of y a curve with a short horizontal?
    Is your upside-down arch the same shape as your arch?
    Are the two sides of your inverted arch parallel?
    Does your inverted arch branch in at the branching line?
    Does the curve of your inverted arch begin and end at the branching line?
    Does the curve of your inverted arch touch the baseline?
    Are your letters the same width as n?
    Do your letters look like the models?

Assessment Questions: Getty-Dubay® Basic Italic Lowercase

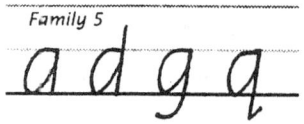

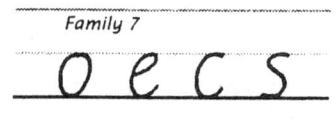

FAMILY 5: BASIC a SHAPE a d g q
    Are you starting at the large dot and following the arrow? (BOOKS A,B,C)
    Do your letters start at the top except d?
    Does your d start at the waistline?
    Do your letters start at the waistline?
    Do your letters start with a horizontal line?
    Does your basic a shape have a horizontal top (flat head) and a soft angle (chin)?
    Do your a and d sit on the baseline?
    Do your g and q end at the descender length?
    Is your descender of g a curve with a short horizontal?
    Does your descender of q end with a sharp angle?
    Do your a, d, g, and q have a straight line downstroke?
    Do your letters branch in at the branching line?
    Are your letters the same width as n?
    Do your letters look like the models?

FAMILY 7: ELLIPTICAL CURVE
    Are you starting at the large dot and following the arrow? (BOOKS A,B,C)
    Do your o, c, and s start at the waistline?
    Does your e start at the branching line?
    Does your e start at the center of the body height?
    Do your c and s start with a horizontal line?
    Does your o look the same right-side-up as upside-down?
    Does your s have a diagonal, like a slide?
    Is your o an ellipse?
    Is your elliptical curve the same for o and e?
    Are you overlapping your o at the waistline?
    Are your o and c the same width as n?
    Is your s slightly narrower than n?
    Do your letters look like the models?

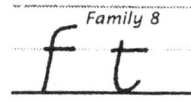

FAMILY 8: CROSSBAR
    Are you starting at the large dot and following the arrow? (BOOKS A,B,C)
    Does your f start at the ascender height?
    Does your f begin with a horizontal blending into a curve to the waistline?
    Do your f and t sit on the baseline?
    Does your t have a short ascender?
    Are you starting t halfway between the ascender height and the waistline?
    Does your t end with a curve at the baseline?
    Are the crossbars of your f and t at the waistline?
    Does the crossbar of your f begin slightly to the left of the downstroke?
    Does the crossbar of your t begin slightly to the left of the downstroke?
    Are your letters the same width as n?

FAMILY 6: INVERTED (UPSIDE-DOWN) BASIC a SHAPE b p
    Are you starting at the large dot and following the arrow? (BOOKS A,B,C)
    Do your letters start at the top?
    Does your b start at the ascender height?
    Does your p end at the descender length?
    Do your b and p start with a straight line downstroke?
    Do your letters branch out at the branching line?
    Are your letters the same width as n?
    Do your letters look like the models?

A quick brown fox jumps over the lazy dog.

GETTY-DUBAY® ITALIC HANDWRITING SERIES
ASSESSMENT QUESTIONS: BASIC ITALIC CAPITALS

Questions pertaining to all basic capitals:

Are you beginning all capitals at the capital height?
Are all of your capitals sitting on the baseline?

Is your A medium width?
Are you making a "tepee" shape to begin A?
Does your horizontal touch the 1st and 2nd strokes?

Is your B narrow width?
Is your 1st stroke of B a straight downstroke?
Does the first curve of the 2nd stroke touch the 1st stroke?

Is your C wide width?
Are you curving up slightly after touching the baseline?

Is your D wide width?
Is your 1st stroke a straight downstroke?

Is your E narrow width?
Is your 1st stroke the shape of capital L?
Are all of your horizontals the same length?

Is your F narrow width?
Is your 1st stroke a straight downstroke?
Are your two horizontals the same length?

Is your G wide width?
Are you beginning the 2nd stroke in the center of the G curve?

Is your H medium width?
Does your horizontal touch the 1st and 2nd strokes?

Is your I narrow width?
Are your horizontals very short lines?

Is your J narrow width?
Are you curving up only slightly from the baseline?

Is your K medium width?
Is your 1st stroke a straight downstroke?
Is your 2nd stroke a right angle turned about 45 degrees from the baseline?

Is your L narrow width?
Is the length of your horizontal about 1/2 the height of your downstroke?

Is your M wide width?
Are you touching the baseline with the V shape?

Is your N medium width?
Is your 1st downstroke a straight line?

Is your O wide width?
Are you overlapping as you finish the O?

Is your P narrow width?
Are you ending the curve slightly below the center of the downstroke?

Is your Q wide width?
Are you overlapping the 1st stroke of Q?

Is your R narrow width?
Are you beginning the 2nd stroke with a short horizontal before curving?

Is your S narrow width?

Is your T medium width?
Is your horizontal centered over the downstroke?

Is your U medium width?
Are you writing U in one stroke?
Are you ending the U with a downstroke to the baseline?

Is your V medium width?

Is your W wide width?
Is the inverted V in the center of W touching the capital height?

Is your X medium width?
Are you beginning your second stroke at the baseline?

Is your Y medium width?

Is your Z medium width?
Are your two horizontals about the same length?

OPTION: The writer may choose to use basic italic capitals with cursive italic lowercase.

Ann Bill Carlos Dana Ellen Fay Greg

GETTY-DUBAY® ITALIC HANDWRITING SERIES
ASSESSMENT QUESTIONS: CURSIVE ITALIC CAPITALS

A — Are you ending your first stroke of A with a curve exit serif?
Are you extending the entrance to the horizontal of A?
Is your horizontal of A on the branching line?

B — Are you beginning your second stroke of B with a curve entrance serif?

C — Does your cursive C look like the basic C?

D — Are you beginning your second stroke of D with a curve entrance serif?

E — Are you beginning your second stroke of E with a curve entrance serif?

F — Are you beginning your second stroke of F with a curve entrance serif?

G — Are you using a one-stroke G?
Are you ending your G with a curve exit serif at the descender length?

H — Are you beginning H with a sharp angle entrance serif?
Are you beginning the curve entrance serif of the second stroke of H slightly higher than the capital height?
Are you extending the entrance to the horizontal of H?

I — Are you beginning your I with a horizontal entrance serif?
Are you ending your I with a horizontal exit serif?

J — Are you beginning your J with a horizontal entrance serif?
Are you ending your J with a curve exit serif at the baseline?

K — Are you beginning your K with a sharp angle entrance serif?
Are you ending your second stroke of K with a curve exit serif?

L — Are you beginning your L with a curve entrance serif?
Are you ending your L with a short exit serif?

M — Are you ending your first stroke of M with a curve exit serif?

N — Are you ending your first stroke of N with a curve exit serif?
Are you beginning the curve entrance serif of the third stroke of N slightly higher than the capital height?

O — Does your cursive O look like the basic O?

P — Are you beginning your second stroke of P with a curve entrance serif?

Q — Are you ending your second stroke of Q with a short exit serif at the descender length?

R — Are you beginning your second stroke of R with a curve entrance serif?
Are you ending your third stroke of R with a curve exit serif?

S — Does your cursive S look like the basic S?

T — Are you beginning the top of your T with a curve entrance serif?

U — Are you beginning your U with a soft angle entrance serif?

V — Are you beginning your V with a curve entrance serif?

W — Are you beginning your W with a curve entrance serif?

X — Are you beginning your X with a curve entrance serif?
Are you ending the first stroke of X with a curve exit serif?

Y — Are you beginning your Y with a soft angle entrance serif? Are you ending your Y with a curve exit serif at the descender length?

Z — Are you beginning your Z with a short entrance serif?
Are you ending your Z with a short exit serif?

ASSESSMENT QUESTIONS: GETTY-DUBAY® CURSIVE ITALIC LOWERCASE JOINS

an
JOIN 1: DIAGONAL
- Are you using a straight diagonal line for the join?
- Are you joining with a diagonal from the baseline into a soft angle entrance serif?
- Are you AVOIDING a wavy line?

au
JOIN 2: DIAGONAL SWING UP
- Are you joining with a diagonal from the baseline to the imaginary branching line?
- Does your diagonal swing up into the letters at the branching line?
- Do you like to jot or dot the i and j?
- Do you like a sharp angle or a soft angle at the bottom of v and w?
- Are you AVOIDING a scoop and loop joining into ascenders?

ao
JOIN 3: DIAGONAL START BACK
- Are you joining with a straight diagonal line from the baseline to the waistline?
- Do you start back down the diagonal into o and s?
- Are you AVOIDING a wave?
- Do you like to leave the top on s when joining, as in Join 8?

ae
JOIN 4: DIAGONAL INTO e
- Are you joining into e at the branching line?
- Are you using a straight diagonal line from the baseline to the center of e?
- Are you AVOIDING a scoop into e?

ou
JOIN 5: HORIZONTAL
- Are you joining out of o with a horizontal line?
- Are you joining out of the crossbar of t and f?
- Are you joining out of o, t, f, v, w, and x at the waistline?
- Are you joining out of o, v, w, and x with a diagonal into e?
- Are you lifting after t and f before e? (See OPTIONS)
- Do you use the optional joins out of f and t into e?

ru
JOIN 6: DIAGONAL OUT OF r
- Are you joining out of r with a short diagonal line?
- Are you joining out of r just below the waistline?
- Are you bending the arm of r at the waistline?
- Are you AVOIDING rn looking like m?
- Are you using the optional pointed arm of r?

su
JOIN 7: HORIZONTAL TO DIAGONAL
- Are you following back out of b, p, and s joining with a diagonal line?
- Are you joining with a horizontal at the baseline into a diagonal?

aa
JOIN 8: DIAGONAL TO HORIZONTAL
- Are you joining with a diagonal from the baseline into a horizontal at the waistline?
- Do you like to keep the top of s rather than leave it off as in Join 3?
- Are you AVOIDING a wave?

af
LIFTS:
- Are you lifting before f?
- Are you lifting before z from the baseline?
- Are you lifting after g, j, q, and y?
- Are you spacing letters close together when lifting?
- Are you AVOIDING a gap between letters in a word?

SIZE: Do your letters have an even body height?

SLOPE:
- Are your letters written with an even slope?
- Are your downstrokes following the slope lines?

SPACING:
- Are your letters close together in words?
- Are you AVOIDING gaps in words?

SPEED:
- Are you writing at a comfortable speed?
- Are you able to increase your written words per minute by one or two words after doing the timed writing exercise?
- Are you able to write faster and keep your writing easy to read?
- Are you able to write faster and keep your writing looking neat?

GETTY-DUBAY® ITALIC HANDWRITING SERIES
ASSESSMENT CHART

Informal Assessment of Student Progress

Use the following categories when evaluating a student's progress in the *Getty-Dubay® Italic Handwriting Series*. This subjective evaluation is to be based on the student's handwriting papers. Student and teacher take into consideration the three types of handwriting:

1) formal—very carefully written papers written during direct instruction, reports, term papers, etc.;
2) informal—daily assignments, rough drafts of poems, stories, etc.;
3) rapid—quickly written lists of in-class and homework assignments, a student's own personal notes, etc.

Essential characteristics of legibility: 0 = Low, 5 = High

1. **Strokes**

    Student knows direction of strokes of lowercase letters

    Student knows direction of strokes of capitals

2. **Shape**

    Student knows and writes basic italic letter shapes of lowercase letters

    Student knows and writes basic italic letter shapes of capitals and numbers

3. **Size**

    Student knows proper size of lowercase letters

    Student knows proper size of capitals

4. **Slope**

    Student writes with a consistent 0–15° letter slope

5. **Spacing**

    Student writes lowercase letters close together within words

    Student writes with appropriate space between lowercase words

6. **Speed**

    Student writes at a reasonable rate for individual ability (see *Timed Writing*, page 61)

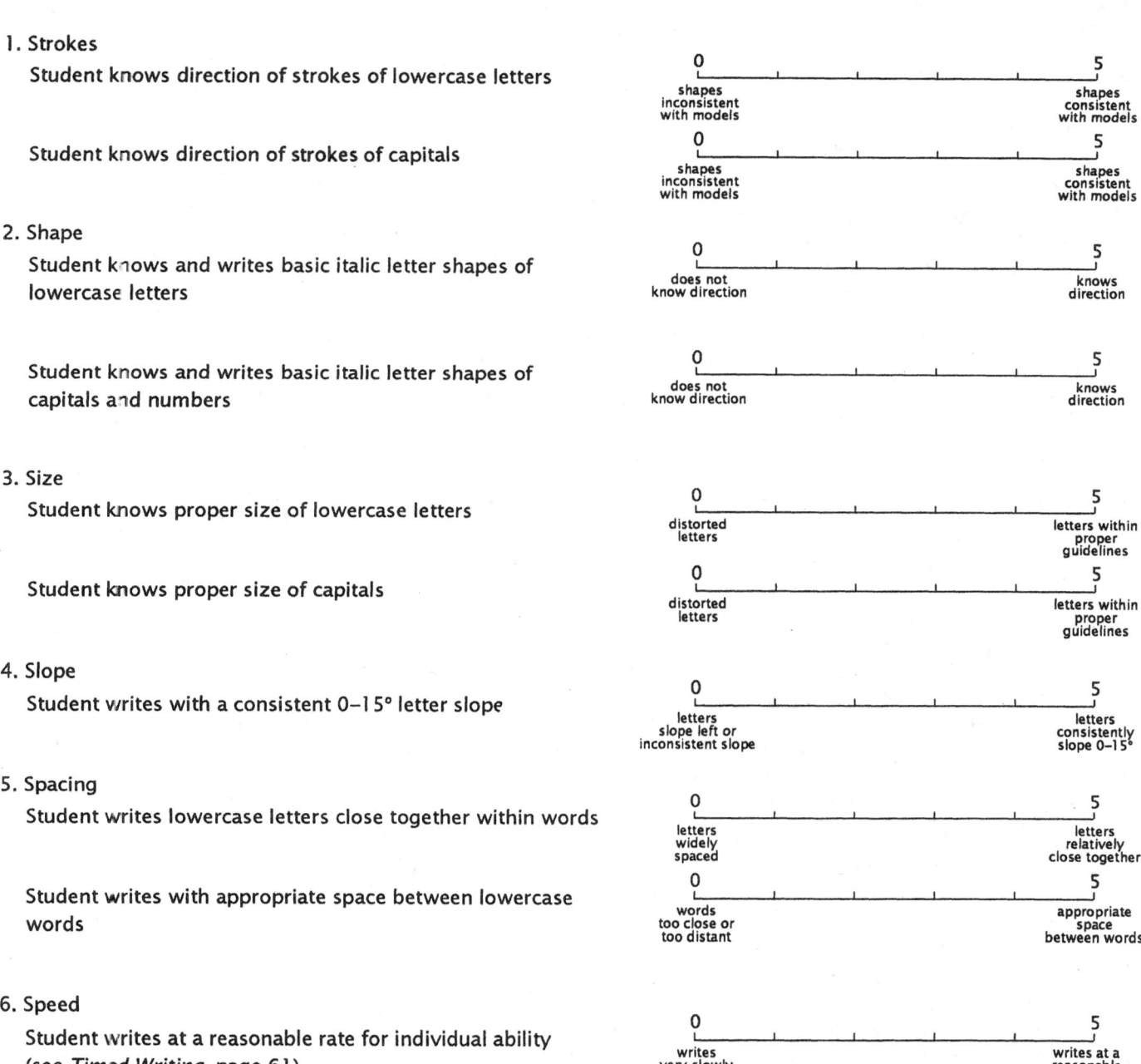

LOOK, PLAN, PRACTICE
Self-assessment in Handwriting Instruction
By Tia Wulff

During my years as an elementary school teacher, my students have taught me much about how to spark their interest and to inspire enthusiasm for excellence.

I feel confident that my students know that my wish is for each of them to succeed. I know that success must be specifically defined, planned for, and often uniquely prescribed for each student. I do not expect students to compete with one another, or for grades. Rather, I want each student to know his/her own strengths and weaknesses, and to know how with optimal effort and awareness to meet the highest standard of personal achievement possible.

Students are able to assume this kind of responsibility. We, as teachers, must teach them how to strive for optimal achievement as well as provide opportunities for them to achieve.

The key ingredients for optimal student achievement are:
1) Clearly defined goals
2) Awareness of the constructs of these goals
3) Proficiency with skills that make the goals attainable
4) Ability to assess one's own progress

If a student knows where he/she is going, success will be more likely. Certainly, practicing the wrong way, without awareness of error, does not lead to learning. Integrating assessment into instruction saves steps for the teacher, as well as providing a learning opportunity otherwise lost to the student. The best situation is one in which the student understands which efforts lead to success, discovering as he/she learns *what* and *how* to assess personal progress. This understanding is further promoted by continually monitoring and redirecting those efforts toward the kind and quality of outcomes desired and appropriate for that individual.

In the *Getty-Dubay® Italic Handwriting Series*, the authors' concern is for specific improvements to be made in handwriting—using the LOOK, PLAN, and PRACTICE process. (See pages 54 and 55.)

Students must know that neat and legible handwriting is the result of shape, size, spacing, and slope, matching the models in the workbook. Each of these letter dimensions has defining features and a unique vocabulary. Also, students develop individual styles of handwriting, as explained in *Options* in the INSTRUCTION MANUAL. A teacher who models the proper letter construction while describing the defining features (using key vocabulary) helps the student's mind and eye discriminate unique features and become aware of his/her own developing style. Thus, the path to success is made clear—enabling the student to analyze his/her own work and to adjust efforts accordingly. Fueled with a clear understanding of how to do well, a student is inspired to succeed.

At first, the teacher will model assessment of handwriting—naming letter qualities in need of improvement and prescribing specific corrections to practice (regularly and before too many mistakes are made). Soon, however, the teacher will jointly define with the student his/her progress *and* plan for further success. Finally, the student will independently assess, prescribe and self-correct efforts toward the goal.

This INSTRUCTION MANUAL offers assessment questions for the student to respond to during handwriting practice. Those questions may be supplemented by others from teacher or student. The essence of assessment questions is always, "What is to be learned and how do I learn it?"

Records of the progress that define *skills gained* are rewarding and useful (e.g., "Size is now even throughout;" "Shapes follow models, except for low branching on the **n**;" "Slope is uniform except for letters with ascenders").

A simple plus, check, and minus code correlating to specific handwriting dimensions may be used for recording progress. Dates on this record will indicate the pace of progress. A student portfolio is a useful record of progress over time highlighting a student's personal best.

When students compare their early handwriting to later accomplishments, they praise themselves and each other in genuine celebration as they recognize and fully understand their improvement.

Tia Wulff has studied with the Assessment Institute at Harvard University and the Assessment Training Institute in Portland, Oregon. She has taught at a public alternative school in Portland, Oregon and is an expert in classroom assessment.

Getty-Dubay® Italic Handwriting Implementation

Implementing the Getty-Dubay® Italic Handwriting Series
Sample Letter to Parents
Two-hour Inservice Outline
Basic & Cursive Lowercase Inservice Page
Cursive Lowercase Joins Inservice Page
Basic & Cursive Capitals Inservice Page

·abcdefghijklmnopqrstuvwxyz·

IMPLEMENTING GETTY-DUBAY® ITALIC HANDWRITING SERIES IN THE ELEMENTARY CLASSROOM

A legible, fluent, and practical handwriting program is an essential part of the elementary school curriculum, and the *Getty-Dubay® Italic Handwriting Series* provides such a program. The decision to implement a new program should involve administrators, teachers, school board members and parents, depending on the way new programs are implemented in your school. Make sure that each group understands the rationale for the change.

Teachers should also know that, although they will have to be able to recognize and model letter shapes, the choice to adapt their own handwriting is voluntary and not required by this program.

As a suggestion, we recommend schools consider sending home a letter, such as the one on page 72, to advise parents of the facts of the changeover and the advantages that will result from the choice of italic.

It is necessary to establish a budget to provide inservice for teachers, textbooks, and supplementary materials, and to make certain administrative support is available for financial and operational needs.

The *Getty-Dubay® Italic Handwriting Series* program may be implemented as a total program, K-6, the first year. If students in grades 4-6 have been using a looped cursive program, the authors recommend Getty-Dubay® in K-3 the first year, increasing one grade level each subsequent year, to ease the presentation of a new cursive form of writing. However, most schools choose italic as a total program to begin with, since many upper elementary students have poor handwriting. Consistency is key, as mixing handwriting styles within a school from grade to grade or classroom to classroom will likely cause confusion and frustration for the students.

Teachers in the upper elementary grades need to be knowledgeable about the fundamentals of the italic style so that they may assist students who still need to improve their skills. Provision should also be made for students who transfer from a school with a different handwriting curriculum. Older students are usually able to rapidly change over to the italic style in the same way that adults can, as long as they are appropriately motivated.

INSERVICE: Arrange an inservice presentation for all teachers. It is helpful if support staff also attend a session. A two-hour inservice outline is provided on page 73 along with three inservice practice pages, 74-76. This writing practice session is essential to ensure teacher confidence in the new program.

Provide teachers with the following materials:
 INSTRUCTION MANUAL *Getty-Dubay®*
  Italic Handwriting Series
 WORKBOOKS–one per student
 WALL CHART
 DESK STRIPS–one per student appropriate to
  grade level
 BLACKLINE MASTERS for each grade level

See pages 6-8 for descriptions of components of the SERIES.

TIME TO TEACH: Handwriting requires direct instruction—how to do it and how to put it to use. Teachers need to provide adequate time in their lesson plans for handwriting instruction. See *Notes to Teachers*, 18-31 for information on BOOKS A-G. The entire section on *Teaching Italic*, 10–52, provides information for a total italic handwriting program.

SUPPORT: Define a clear strategy for educating teachers and parents. Build awareness of the importance of a strong handwriting program. As with any educational agenda, enthusiasm and support are important in providing an effective and rewarding program.

PARENTS & CAREGIVERS: It is important to assure parents that their children will be able to read handwriting of other family members, and vice versa.

Provide parents with inservice pages 74-76 and/or desk strips.

Ways parents can help children with handwriting:

a) Young children need to know what printed language stands for and how it is used to communicate. Don't assume they know. Provide examples of "talk written down": books, pictures with labels, maps, signs, product packaging, envelopes to be mailed, newspapers, magazines, computers.

To aid letter perception for the young student:

b) Help student give accurate verbal descriptions of things he/she sees.

c) Help student form letters by demonstrating, one at a time, the direction letters go—then have child write them. Proceed according to alphabet "families" or in alphabetical order.

d) Encourage student to look at the finished letters and words after writing them.

Student writing tools:

e) Supply standard pencil, pen, chalk, felt-tip marker (usually a favorite), and crayon.

Tool hold:

f) Check the amount of tool pressure on the paper. Encourage student to write with more or less pressure if lines are too light or too dark.

g) If student holds the tool too tightly, he/she may be uncomfortable and may not write for long.

h) To determine if the student is tense, check to see if his/her teeth are clenched. If so, help child relax.

Teacher and parents through their support and praise can be instrumental in building the student's self-confidence and pride which naturally tends to follow the acquisition of a legible and neat italic hand.

SAMPLE LETTER
FOR PARENTS OF STUDENTS USING GETTY-DUBAY® ITALIC HANDWRITING SERIES

Dear Parent,

Your child is learning a handwriting style that will become a lifelong skill—italic handwriting. Italic offers numerous advantages over the other handwriting programs most of us were taught:

- Italic has no loops—a major cause of illegibility.
- Italic builds on previously learned concepts, so it builds a solid base of skills.
- It's logical—there is no frustrating transition in letter shapes from printing to cursive.
- The letters are elliptical and conform to natural hand movements.
- Italic encourages self-esteem and success because progress and accomplishment are rapid and results are often praised.
- Italic remains legible, even when written rapidly.

As you can see, basic and cursive italic letterforms are essentially the same:

This is a sample of basic italic.
This is a sample of cursive italic.

After learning to print, your child will learn cursive by simply joining the letters already learned.

If you would like suggestions on ways to help your child, ask his/her teacher to provide you with a copy of page 71 from the *Getty-Dubay® Italic Handwriting Series Instruction Manual*. In addition, creative handwriting activities that you and your child can do together can be found on pages 78-85 of the same manual. In this way, you can support and encourage your child as he/she progresses through this exciting time of handwriting acquisition.

If you have any questions concerning our program, please feel free to contact me.

Sincerely,

TWO-HOUR INSERVICE
GETTY-DUBAY® ITALIC HANDWRITING SERIES

INTRODUCTION (3 minutes) Note: times are approximate, alter as necessary
- Importance of handwriting as a necessary skill for daily living
- Importance of legibility--we write to be read, mostly by others
- Importance of italic as a viable alternative to looped cursive
  (illustrate clarity of cursive italic vs. looped cursive)

REMINDERS (4 minutes)
- correct posture
- paper hold for left- and right-handed students
- convenient pencil/pen holds–"tapping forefinger to establish comfortable hold"
- relaxation of body and hand (research indicates more legible writing occurs when relaxed)

VOCABULARY (4 minutes) refer to chart at bottom of inservice sheet #1
- point out need for consistency, then demonstrate vocabulary as follows:
- baseline, waistline, body height ("x" height), ascender, descender,
- capital height, branching line, counter, downstroke, diagonal, arch,
- inverted arch, crossbar, etc.

ASSESSMENT (4 minutes)
- shape; size; slope; spacing within words and between words; stroke sequence (then address building speed, BOOK D and beyond)

ITALIC HANDWRITING SERIES overview (3 minutes)
- show 2 overlays from each book, giving audience an introduction to the program; also show wall charts, desk strips, blackline masters

BASIC ITALIC AND CURSIVE ITALIC FAMILIES (25 minutes)
- 1. ijl 2. kvwxz 3. hmnr 4. uy 5. adgq 6. bp 7. oecs 8. ft
- Writing hints: writing in air, individually in cornmeal, on chalkboard(students and teachers); writing with eyes closed

BASIC AND CURSIVE ITALIC CAPITAL FAMILIES (12 minutes)
(Note: We read and write capitals approximately 2% of the time)
- 1. CGOQD (wide)
- 2. MW (widest)
- 3. AHKNTUVXYZ (4/5 as wide as high)
- 4. EFIL: straight lines and BPRSJ: curved lines (approximately half as wide as high)
- Review these quickly with an introduction to the capital serifs

BREAK (10 minutes)

SENTENCE WRITING A quick brown fox jumps over the lazy dog. (5 minutes)

CURSIVE ITALIC JOINS (25 minutes)
Practice a word or two after introducing each join.
- 1. Diagonal join - into m, n, r, x (Dan, Kim, Mar, Lex)
- 2. Diagonal swing up - into b, h, i, j, k, l, p, t, u, v, w, y (Lei, Matt, Bev) Option: n, m, r, x
- 3. Diagonal start back - into o, s (Julio, Linus)
- 4. Diagonal into e - (Anne, Melei, Alex, Umeko)
- 5. Horizontal join - out of o, t, f, v, w, x (Lois, Otto, Cliff, Yvonne)
- 6. Diagonal join - out of r (Chris, Erin Karim, Mary)
- 7. Horizontal to diagonal - out of b, p, s (Ashley, Makesi, Susie, Jessie)
- 8. Diagonal to horizontal - into a, c, d, g, q, s (Diana, Omar, Barbara, Papa)

Reminder: Lift before f and z; lift after g, j, q, and y. Exception: may use horizontal join into z

NUMERALS 0-9 (5 minutes)

SENTENCE WRITING with joins: A quick brown fox jumps over the lazy dog. (10 minutes)

HANDWRITING PROJECT IDEAS (5 minutes)

CLOSING (5 minutes)

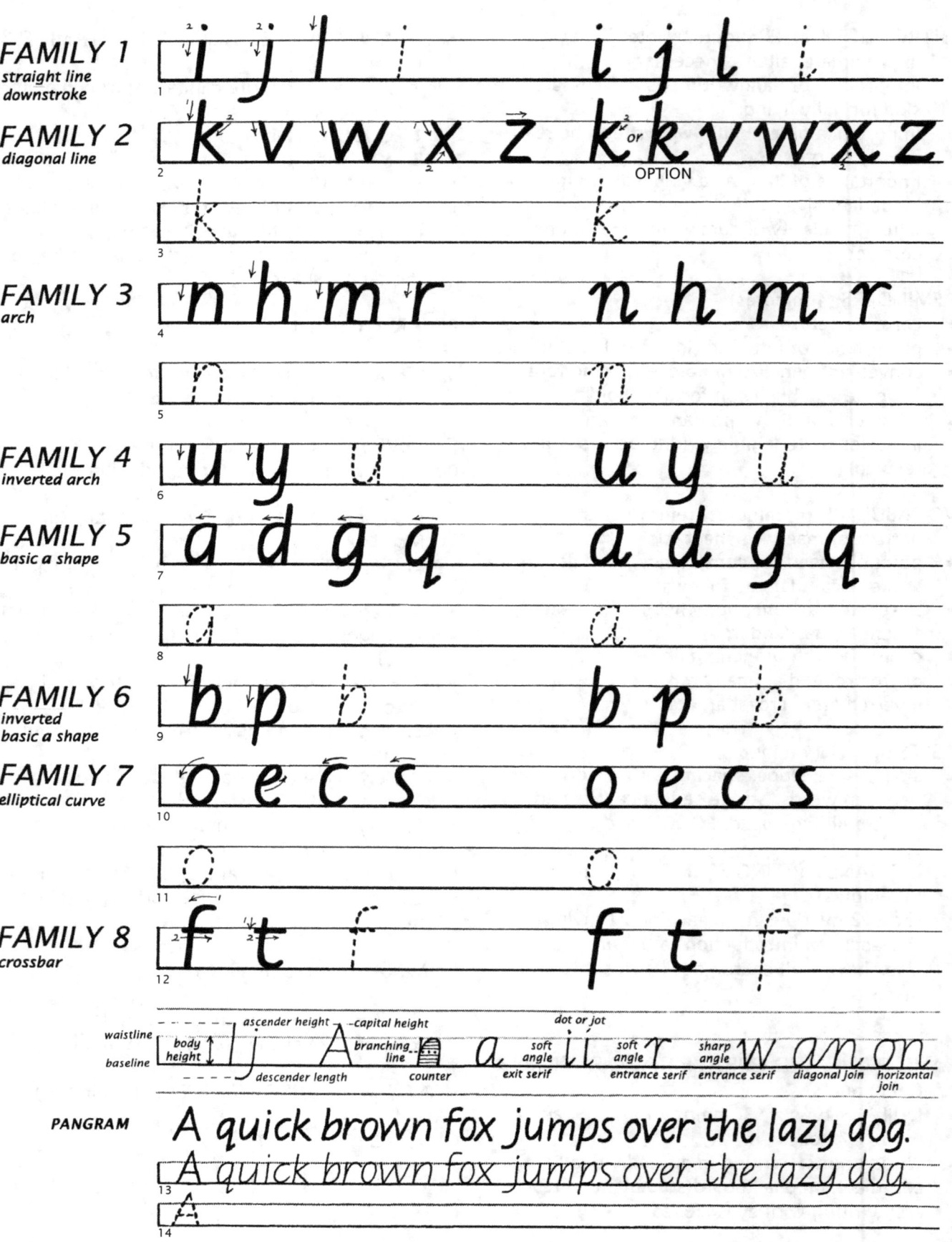

GETTY-DUBAY® ITALIC HANDWRITING SERIES
INSERVICE: CURSIVE ITALIC LOWERCASE JOINS

JOIN 1
diagonal
an am an

ar ax ar

JOIN 2
diagonal swing up
an am ar ax an
OPTION

au ay ai at au

aj ap av aw aj

at ah ab ak or ak at
OPTION

JOIN 3
diagonal start back
ao as ao
OPTION

JOIN 4
diagonal into e
ae ee ie ue ae
or lift after e

JOIN 5
horizontal
on tr th fr on

vi wi xi vi

JOIN 6
diagonal out of r
rn ri ro ra re rt rn
or lift after r

JOIN 7
horizontal to diagonal
sn br pr sn
or lift after s, b, p

JOIN 8
diagonal to horizontal
aa ac ad aa
or lift before a, c, c, g, q, s

ag aq as ag
OPTION

LIFTS
af az gu ju qu yu

PANGRAM
A quick brown fox jumps over the lazy dog.
A quick brown fox jumps over the lazy dog.

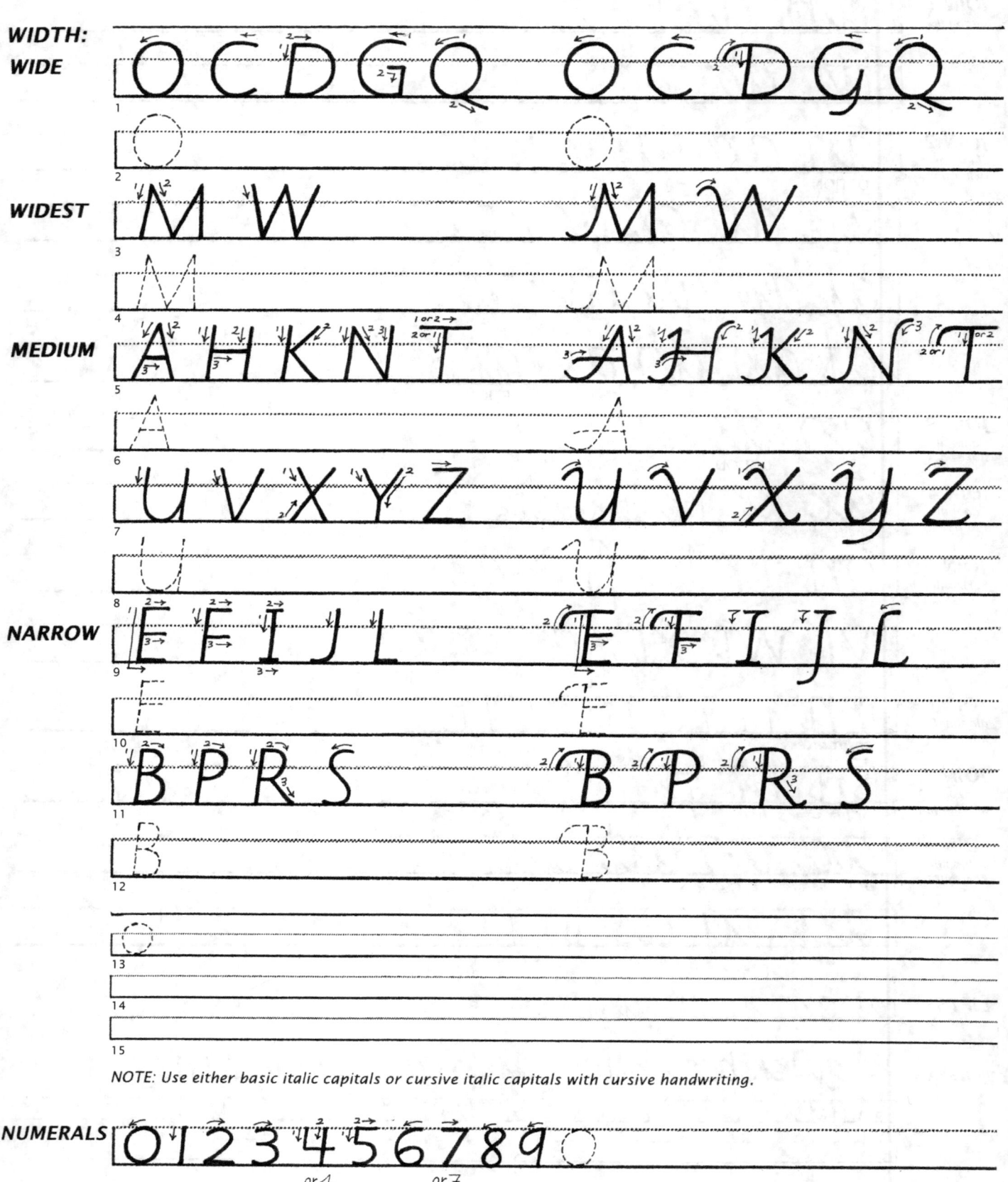

Getty-Dubay® Activities/Supplements

Handwriting Activities and Projects
Development of the Alphabet
Glossary
Bibliography

GETTY-DUBAY® ITALIC HANDWRITING SERIES
HANDWRITING ACTIVITIES AND PROJECTS

1. **Alphabet books**—student writes capital and/or lowercase letter, then word/sentence; draw or cut out picture to go with each letter; student designs cover, may also hand stitch booklet (see pp. 81–82).

2. **Greeting cards** for all occasions (see p. 80).

3. Unit on **letter writing** to friends, businesses, famous personalities, telling, describing, asking, explaining, exclaiming, thanking, etc.

4. **Envelope** addressing—ways to design an attractive envelope (be sure the state and zip are written on the same line).

5. **Labels** for all uses—have students name various ways we label things, then write out labels suitable for each person; self-sticking labels come in all sizes!

6. **Books**—write own short stories, poems or copy favorites written by others.

7. Design **title pages** of own books or of a favorite story.

8. Design own **bookplate**—"This book belongs to . . ."

9. Write your **own name**—use as a pattern, written small, for a border design; "How many other ways can you use your name?"

10. **Calligrams**—shaped writing; use letters of a word to form a picture of that word or use a sentence or a short story about a form, for example, a fish, then form a fish with the words.

11. **Weathergrams**—as suggested in Lloyd Reynolds' booklet entitled, "*Weathergrams.*" Write a short "haiku-like" phrase about life, with a felt pen or edged pen on a piece of grocery bag paper. Tie to a tree with string and let the words weather.

12. See *Fun With Pens*, a Pentalic book by Christopher Jarman, with many ideas about using words and letters. Written for the edged pen, but ideas can also be used with pencil, ball point and felt pens.

13. **Write to music**—don't try to keep time with it, but let it help relax your mind and your hand. Write what you want—your own words, a favorite saying, a short story, lyrics of a song, etc.

14. Write on different **textures of paper**—paper toweling, napkins, construction paper, anything you can find. Write the same message on each and feel how the texture of the paper changes how fast you write, etc., or does it remain exactly the same?

15. If you have **colored inks** available, mix two together to design your own color. Mix colors of the same brand.

16. Student folds sheet of paper as shown, then writes a letter or word/words beginning with the sound the letter stands for. Student may use butcher paper or construction paper for painting large letters and pictures. It's fun for children to explore many writing materials. For this activity or others, try chalk, felt pens, crayons, soft pencils, hard pencils, etc. Each material feels different when it meets paper.

17. For upper grades and older—design a **monogram** using your own initials. Carve them in reverse (transfer your design with carbon paper onto the eraser), then print from a stamp pad. Cut out your design with an X-acto knife or a small linoleum gouge.

18. Primary grades—design a **color booklet**—write each color word with a crayon of that color. Illustrate.

19. **Recipe** booklet—have each student bring a favorite recipe, then write out on a ditto or on a plain sheet of paper (if a copy machine is available). Illustrate. Teacher does the writing in kindergarten and early grade one. The student draws a picture. This makes a treasure to send home and provides some new recipes for everyone!

20. Practice writing in a **straight line**—place random dots on a piece of paper. Write from one dot to the next. To check how straight you're writing, lift page to eye level and check. You can even design a letter of the alphabet as you write! (This idea is from Fran Sloan.)

21. Write with **colored chalk**, felt pens, paint brushes, etc.

22. Write alphabetical **lists of categories**, such as: names, rivers, lakes, cities, capital cities, states, countries, methods of transportation, animals, fruits, trees, flowers, insects, occupations, etc.

23. Project lines on chalkboard using an **overhead projector**, then let students write one or two at a time.

Getty-Dubay® Handwriting Activities and Projects

24. Read *Drawing On the Right Side of the Brain* by Betty Edwards—a course in enhancing creativity and artistic confidence. You can use her techniques to help students build awareness.

25. If you teach sixth grade or beyond and your students have not used BOOK F of the Series, designed for the fifth grade, you will find it contains **figures of speech**. Over a period of time, write each of them on the board, have students copy and then have them find their own examples—a handwriting and English assignment combined. The figures of speech include: acronyms, euphemisms, mnemonics, maxims, oxymora, pangrams, and others.

26. BOOK E of the Series, designed for the fourth grade, has handwriting samples based on the animal, plant and mineral kingdoms and may provide you with some ideas for handwriting **review** if you teach fifth grade or beyond.

27. On a master sheet draw lines to form 2 rectangles (AB) about 12mm (1/2") apart. Write in at least one sample letter in the **border**, then run copies. Students complete border with letters or words of their choosing or as the group chooses. You may complete activity with your students using an overhead transparency.

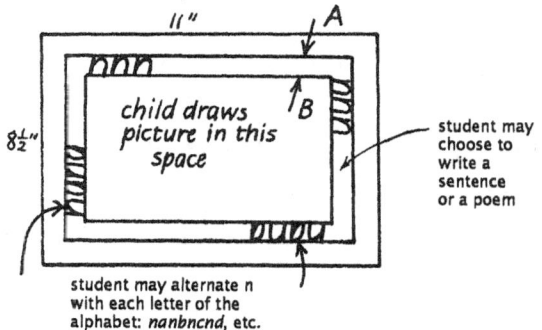

28. Increasing handwriting **speed**—see exercise "*Timed Writing*" on page 61.

29. If you're going to teach kids how to write, they need **ideas**—and these ideas they put down in HANDWRITING! For many ideas to handwrite, beg, borrow or purchase: *If You're Trying To Teach Kids How To Write, You've Gotta Have This Book!* It's written by Marjorie Frank (1979 Incentive Publications, Inc).

30. The **classroom newspaper**—have students write and design a classroom newspaper and reproduce it inexpensively. Send it home once a week or, at least, every two weeks. Give all students an opportunity to contribute—and you, as the teacher, can have your own short column. Co-author Barbara Getty had a classroom newspaper for 14 years and believed it to be an excellent public relations tool. Kids love to see their names in print—especially when it's their own handwriting and their own news or classroom news. Parents enjoy it, too. It does NOT have to be elaborate—don't spend a lot of time on it. Just make certain all words are spelled correctly. Do it and you'll enjoy the results!

31. **Pen pals** — write letters to students in another state, province or country — anywhere they read English. Children and adults studying English as a second language often enjoy corresponding with students in your country.

32. Make a **Magic Writing Slate**. Put good handwriting skills at your students' fingertips with this reusable device made from a ziplock freezer-strength plastic bag. Put finger paint inside the bag, seal it, and reinforce all four edges with masking tape. Kids then use their fingers to "write" on the clean plastic surface, erasing mistakes with a quick flick of the wrist.

33. **Decorated letter** for primary grades: Choose a letter. The teacher makes a large letter on the chalkboard, then the student makes one on paper and decorates it. Tell the student to fill up the entire sheet with decorations.

34. Grades 1-3: "**Pick a Letter**." Have the student pick a favorite letter. Find the letter page in the workbook, then write a large letter on paper. Fill the page with words that have the letter in them. Use words in the workbook or any other words using the favorite letter. Then have the student use some of the words he/she has written to write a sentence. If time permits, have the student draw a picture about the sentence. This activity is illustrated in BOOK B.

35. **Word Picture**. Make a shape with words. Don't outline the form, but use similar size letters to create the shape. To form a tree, use the word "tree" to design the tree, "trunk" to form the trunk, "grass" to form the grass, etc., writing each word over and over and over.

36. Write your **name** or other words on butcher paper with a large (1" or wider) paint brush using tempera paint. Decorate the counters of the letters (the spaces inside them), or make a decorative border design out of two or three letters. Use a smaller brush for the border design.

37. For other **activities** see pages 80–85.

Getty-Dubay® Handwriting Activities and Projects

WAYS TO USE GETTY-DUBAY® ITALIC

GREETING CARD – birthday, get well, friendship, anniversary, etc.
To make a greeting card for a business size envelope, 10.5cm x 24cm (4 1/8 x 8 1/2 in), you will need:
- scissors   • yarn or thread, 90cm (35 1/2 in)   • needle   • ruler   • paperclips
- 1 sheet typing paper (or similar) cut to 19cm x 22cm (7 1/2 in x 8 3/4 in) for inside of card
- 1 sheet colored paper (heavier than typing) cut to 20cm x 23cm (8 x 9 in) for cover of card

a. Fold both sheets lengthwise and crease.
b. Insert typing paper inside cover.
c. Paperclip sheets together.
d. On the inside, make a center dot A and one on either side at equal distances from the center, BC.
e. Push needle through the 3 dots ABC to establish stitching holes.
f. Stitch sheets together as follows:
  1) From outside cover, pass needle through center hole A, leaving 15cm (6 in) for tying.
  2) From inside, pass needle through hole B to outside of card.
  3) From outside, skip over A, pass needle through third hole C to inside.
  4) From inside, pass needle through center hole A to outside.
  5) Tie knot over the long stitch. Cut ends to 4 or 5cm (approximately 1 1/2 or 2 in); or instead of cutting ends, tie in bow as shown.
g. Complete cover and inside message before or after stitching.

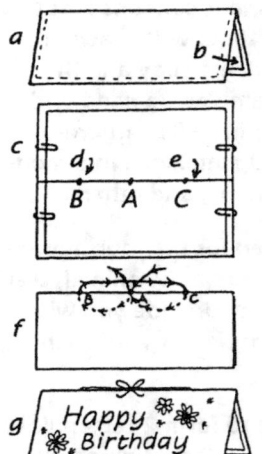

SMALL BOOK
Add a few more inside pages as in illustration b. You may fold all of your sheets either direction: 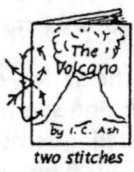 or .

two stitches   four stitches

The four-stitch bookbinding is a bit stronger – tighten each stitch as you go along. Decorate your cover with a drawing, potato print, etc.

ENVELOPE

NOTICE

LETTER

COVER

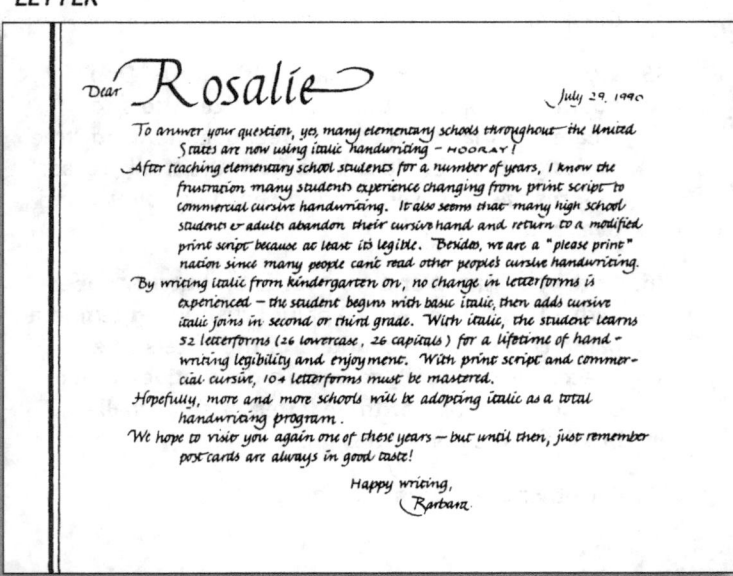

Getty-Dubay® Handwriting Activities and Projects

LETTER/BOOKLET

Write a letter to a relative, a friend, or a pen pal.

ROUGH DRAFT: Compose your letter in pencil.

CHECK WORDING: Edit for capitals, spelling and punctuation.

SURPRISE
BOOKLET: Materials: sheet of light or medium weight paper and scissors. A 28 cm x 43 cm (11" x 17") sheet will give a finished size of 10.8 cm x 14 cm (4 1/4" x 5 1/2"). This size will fit an A-2 envelope.

NOTE: In illustrations dotted line indicates fold that occurs within the given step. Solid lines within rectangle indicate folds previously established.

1. Fold AB to CD to establish EF.
2. Open back to original size.
3. Fold AC to BD to establish GH.
4. Fold GH to AC/BD to establish IJ.
5. Open to previous fold (GH/AB/CD).
6. With scissors, cut KL by cutting halfway between GH, stopping at fold IJ.
7. Open to original size ABCD.
8. Refold AB to CD as in #1.
9. Grasp E/AC with left hand and F/BD with right hand, then push hands together, establishing 3 pages on one side and 1 on the other.
10. Fold remaining leaf over the other three pages. Two leaves have folds at the top and two on the fore edge of the booklet.

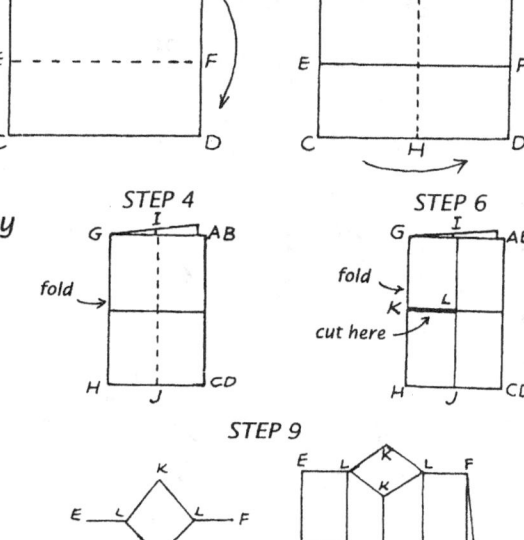

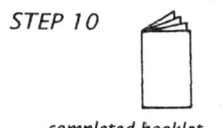

STEP 10
completed booklet

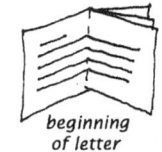
beginning of letter

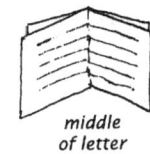
middle of letter

end of letter

Arrange letter on the three two-page spreads of the letter/card. Leave a one inch margin on all sides. Decorate the cover with a design, perhaps using the name of the person the letter is for.

FINAL COPY: Use your best handwriting for your final copy. Take your time. Write your final copy with a pencil or pen.

ENVELOPE: Address the envelope using your best handwriting. On the **first line**, write the name of the person to whom you are writing. On the **second line**, write the person's house number and street name (or P.O. Box number). Add an apartment number, office number, etc. as needed. On the **third line**, write the city, state or province, and postal code. Add country if mailing overseas.

NOTE: Envelope pattern, see page 108

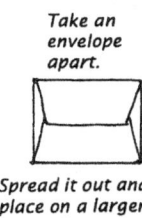
Take an envelope apart.

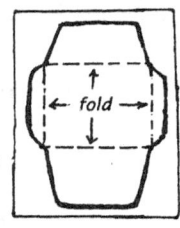
Spread it out and place on a larger piece of paper.

Trace around the edge. Cut out the new envelope. Fold envelope. Glue or tape to hold together.

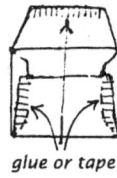
glue or tape

In the upper left hand corner write your return address.

ITALIC LETTERS: Calligraphy and Handwriting

SIMPLE HANDSEWN BOOK
The simple handsewn book can be a useful place to keep notes, write a journal, or keep other handwritten information. It can be used as a gift with quotations, stories, or poems written out on its pages.

Begin with 8 sheets of 8½" x 11" bond paper. (8 sheets will make a 32-page book.) Fold each sheet in half and place one inside the other. This group of sheets is called a signature. Choose a heavier weight paper (cover stock) for the cover—8½" x 11¼". Fold and place outside signature. Secure group of sheets with paper clips or clothespins. Poke 5 holes at the spine with an awl or darning needle, first one in the center, then two other holes evenly spaced on either side. Sew as shown with thread & darning needle.

Be sure thread is pulled taut and that beginning & ending thread are on either side of center thread (5). Then make square knot. Trim ends of thread to an inch or so.

THE CANON · DESIGN FOR 2-PAGE SPREAD · TEXT AREA & MARGINS

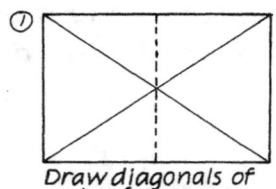
① Draw diagonals of unit of 2 pages.

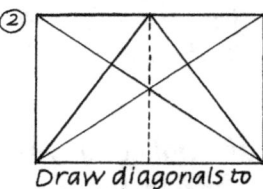
② Draw diagonals to top center.

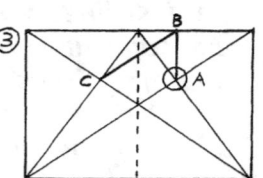
③ From intersection of 2 diagonals on right (A) draw perpendicular line from A to B, then connect to intersection of diagonals on left at C.

④ Point at which BC line intersects diagonal of right side establishes top, side and bottom margins.

This page design for books was used throughout the late Middle Ages and early Renaissance. It was rediscovered by Jan Tschichold, a Swiss designer. It can be worked on any vertical format.

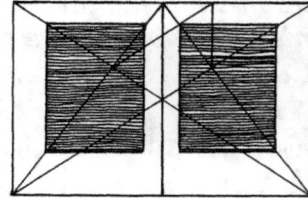

Note gutter margin (center) is the same width as the side margins and the bottom margin is twice the height of the top margin.

Text area of 2-page spread (shaded area)

From: *Italic Letters: Calligraphy & Handwriting*, Inga Dubay & Barbara Getty, 1992, page 118.

CHAPTER X · Design

THE ACCORDION BOOK

The accordion book design originated in the Orient and is composed of a continuous folded sheet of paper enclosed between 2 covers. It may be constructed in any size – from very small to very large – and is a handsome design for a booklet or a special greeting card.

SUPPLIES
- cover board (cardboard, poster board, illustration board)
- cloth or paper for cover
- adding machine tape or pieces of paper joined to make a long strip
- ribbon or cord for ties
- library paste, gluestick, Sobo, or white water-soluble glue (diluted)
  (Avoid rubber cement as it comes through the paper after several months.)

PROCEDURE
- Determine spacing of message on rough draft to determine length of strip.
- Fold strip in equal sections – use any EVEN number of rectangles or squares.
- Write final copy.

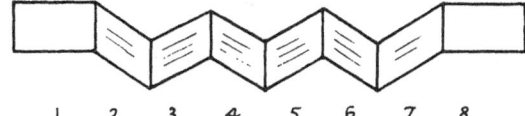

- Cut 2 covers ⅛" to ¼" larger on all sides than folded strip.
  (When working with children, use ¼" to ½" larger covers on all sides for ease in handling.)
- Cut 2 pieces of cloth or paper for cover ½" to ⅝" larger on all sides than the cover board.
- Apply glue to cover board & attach cloth or paper to each board.
- Miter corners, then glue & overlap edges – steps 1, 2, and 3ᵃ or 3ᵇ.

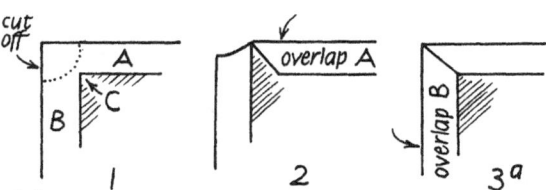

Note: Curve corner when cutting, but do **not** cut to corner (C), or a cloth corner will fray.

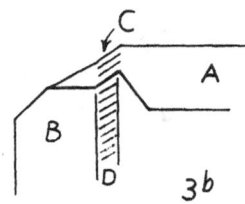

For a neater finish, press mitered edge of paper or fabric around edge of cover board (D) to cover corner completely.

- Glue ribbon across horizontal center of inside of back cover.
- Glue last rectangle of accordion pages to the inside of back cover over the ribbon – leave an equal cover margin on all 4 sides.
- Glue front cover to first rectangle, carefully squaring it with back cover. (If cover design has directional pattern, match before gluing.)

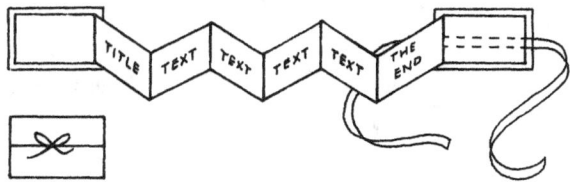

119

From: Italic Letters: Calligraphy & Handwriting, Inga Dubay & Barbara Getty, 1992, page 119.

SPIRAL WRITING

For an unusual design for a letter, try a spiral!

Find the center of sheet (a quick way: fold in half and crease lightly) and draw a line horizontally at center. Establish A at center of line. One-half inch to the right of A, establish B.

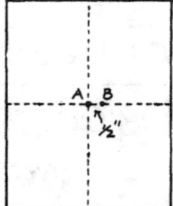
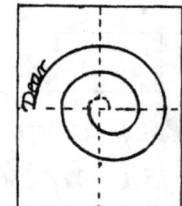

Use your spiral as a liner sheet, placing your stationery over it. Begin at the edge or in the center. For a tighter spiral use less space between A and B.
Add a waistline if needed.

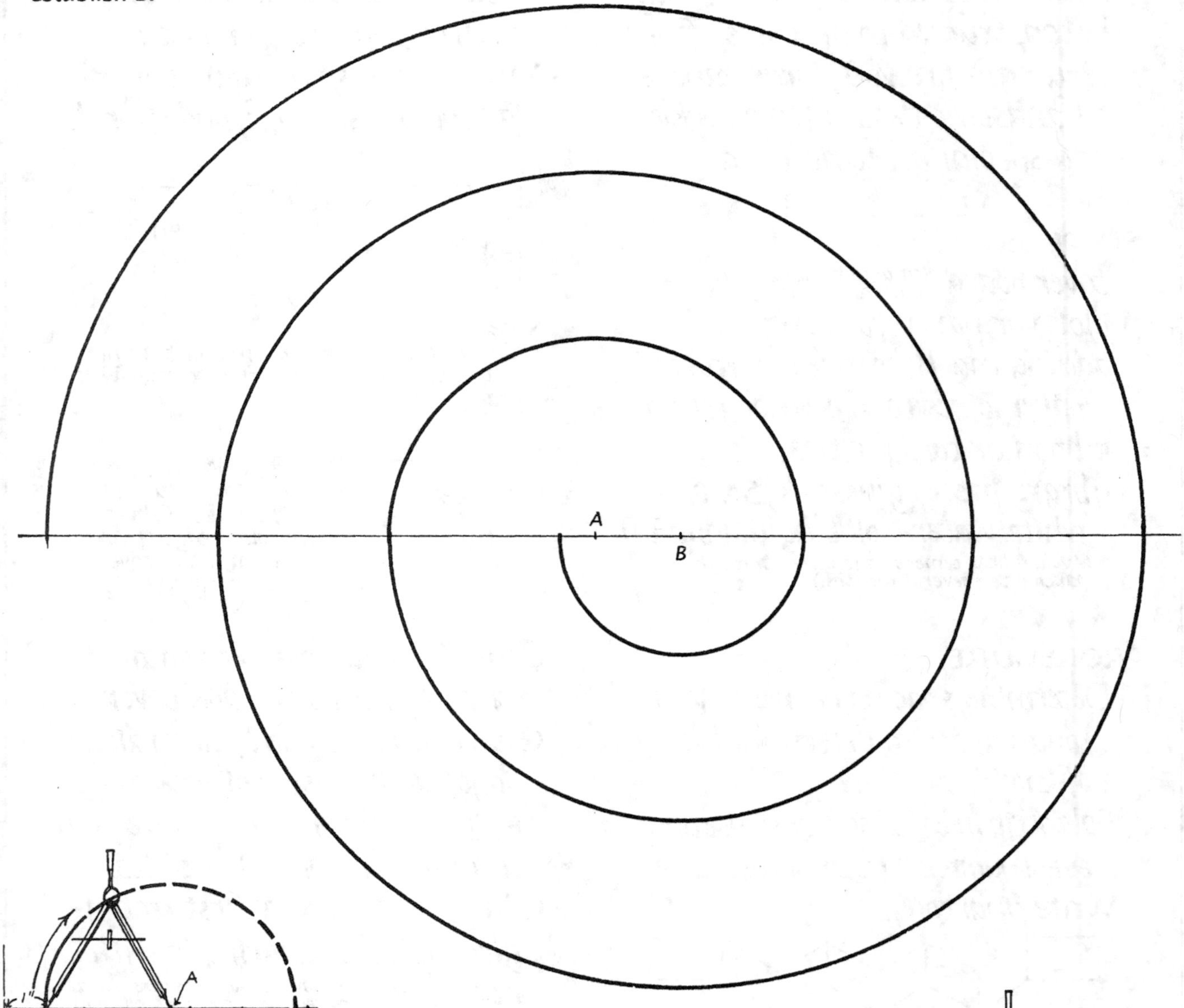

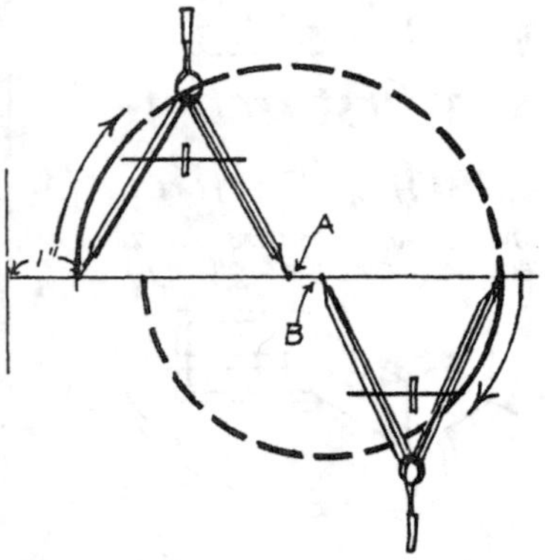

Place point of compass at A and the lead of compass an inch or so from the left edge of paper, and draw a semicircle on top half of sheet.

Next, move point of compass to B and line up lead of compass with line just drawn (tighten compass slightly to adjust). Each semicircle on the top has A as its center, and each semicircle on the bottom has B as its center. Continue spiral to center.

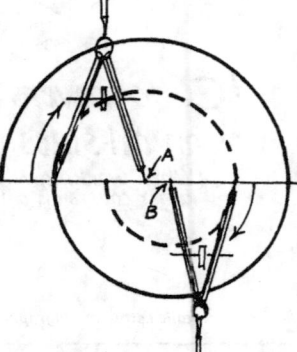

POP-UPS

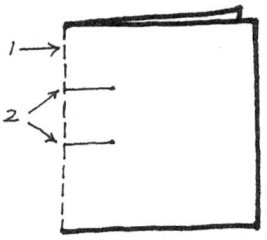

STEP
1. Fold paper in half.
2. Cut two parallel lines of equal length across fold.
3. Fold back area between parallel lines.
4. Unfold to original position and open card. Bring fold forward by reversing fold to form step inside card.
5. Attach image on one side of step. Check size when folded flat to see if it fits inside closed card.

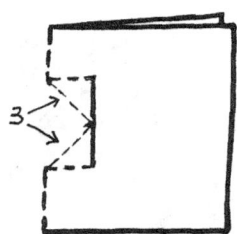

BEAKS & MOUTHS
1. Fold paper in half.
2. Cut one line across fold.
3. Fold back two triangles so cut edges are parallel to edge of card.
4. Unfold to original position and open card. Bring triangle shapes forward by reversing folds to form beak inside card.
5. Add rest of face, words, or vary edges of beak or mouth.

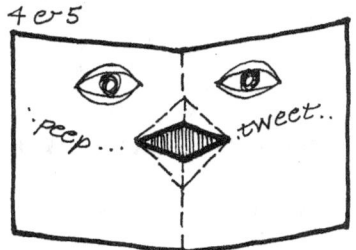

MULTIPLE STEPS
1. Fold paper in half.
2. Cut sets of parallel lines as in the STEP pop-up above. Have a shape in mind, such as a tree shape. Keep cuts less than half the width of a closed card.
3. Fold back each step.
4. Unfold to original position and open card. Bring folds forward by reversing folds to form steps inside card.
5. Attach images on sides of steps, such as birds or decorations.

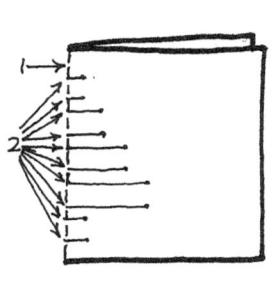

BACKING SHEET
Use a backing sheet to complete the card. Cut and fold a piece of paper the same size as the card. Place this backing sheet behind the card. Fold card closed. Put glue on the back of the card around the edge and around any cuts made. Press backing sheet to glued side of the card. Glue the other side in the same way. The backing sheet could be a similar color, a different color or a decorated sheet.

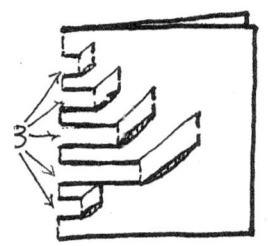

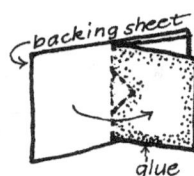

With thanks to Bonnie Stahlecker, Plainfield, Indiana, for Pop-up ideas.

DEVELOPMENT OF THE ALPHABET

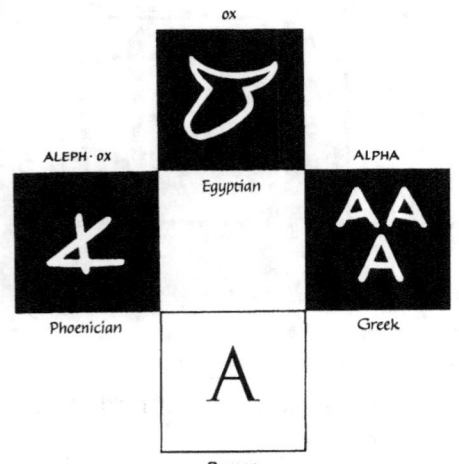

Egyptian hieroglyph representing "ox"
Phoenician letter ∀ name ALEPH "ox"
Early Greek name ALPHA A RIGHT TO LEFT   A LEFT TO RIGHT
←>∀A Boustrophēdon, Greek "ox turning" Lines change
→A∀← direction alternately. After c.500 BCE left to right only.
Classical Greek A
Early Roman A; Imperial Roman A

DEVELOPMENT OF LOWERCASE A

λ λ ɑ ɑ ɑ ɑ a
Rustic Uncial Half-Uncial Carolingian Gothic Humanist Italic

Aa Aa
Basic Italic   Cursive Italic

Egyptian hieroglyphs ▢ ▢ ▢ "house"
Phoenician letter 𐤁 name BETH "house"
Early Greek name BETA 𐤁 RIGHT TO LEFT   B LEFT TO RIGHT
Classical Greek B
Early Roman B; Imperial Roman B

DEVELOPMENT OF LOWERCASE B

b B b b b b b
Rustic Uncial Half-Uncial Carolingian Gothic Humanist Italic

Bb Bb
Basic Italic   Cursive Italic

Phoenician letter ⌐ name GIMEL "camel"
Early Greek > RIGHT TO LEFT < LEFT TO RIGHT
Classical Greek Γ
Early Roman C
Imperial Roman C

The Romans added a bar to C to form G in order to differentiate sounds. G was added to the alphabet in the 3rd century BCE.

Early Roman G
Imperial Roman G

DEVELOPMENT OF LOWERCASE C

C c c c c c c
Rustic Uncial Half-Uncial Carolingian Gothic Humanist Italic

Cc Cc
Basic Italic   Cursive Italic

DEVELOPMENT OF LOWERCASE G

G ɕ ʒ ʒ ɡ g
Rustic Uncial Half-Uncial Carolingian Gothic Humanist Italic

Gg Gg
Basic Italic   Cursive Italic

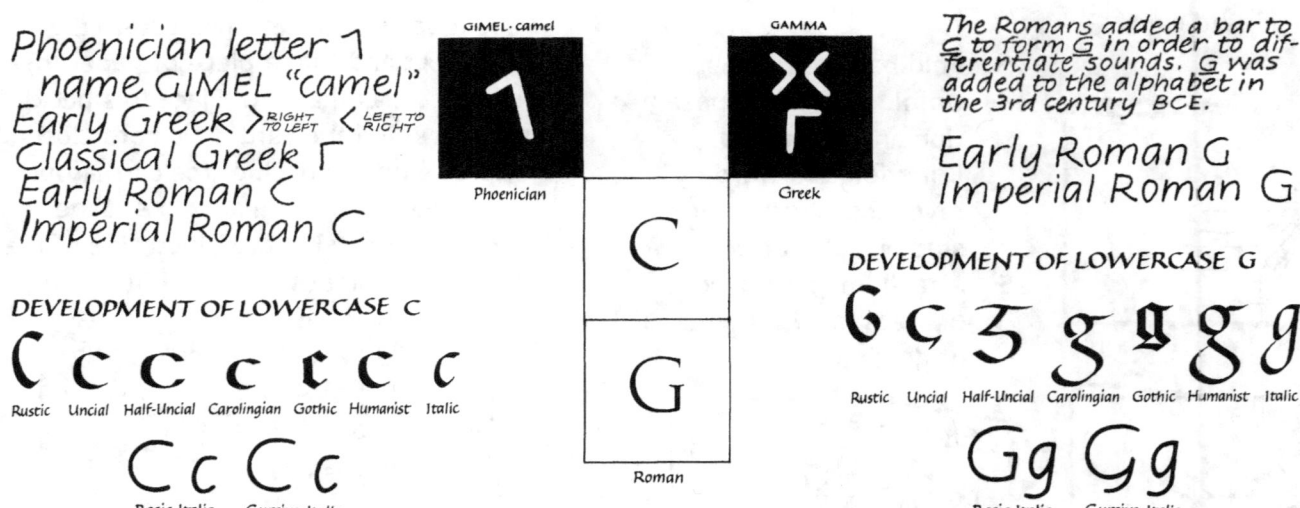

The development of the alphabet is based on ANCIENT WRITING AND ITS INFLUENCES by Berthold Louis Ullman

Development of the Alphabet

Egyptian hieroglyph ⊞ representing "door"
Phoenician letter △ name DALETH "door"
Early Greek name DELTA ◁ RIGHT TO LEFT D LEFT TO RIGHT
Classical Greek △
Early Roman D; Imperial Roman D

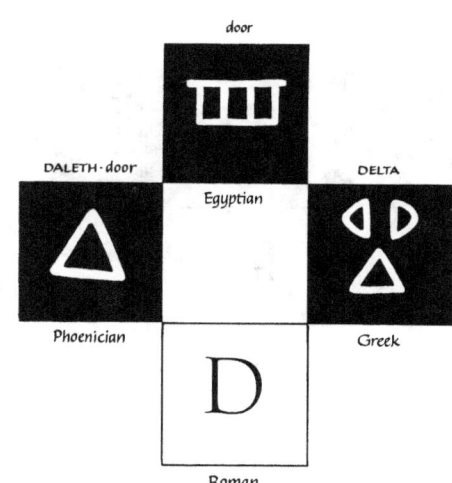

DEVELOPMENT OF LOWERCASE D

D ɒ d d d d
Rustic Uncial Half-Uncial Carolingian Gothic Humanist Italic

Dd Dd
Basic Italic Cursive Italic

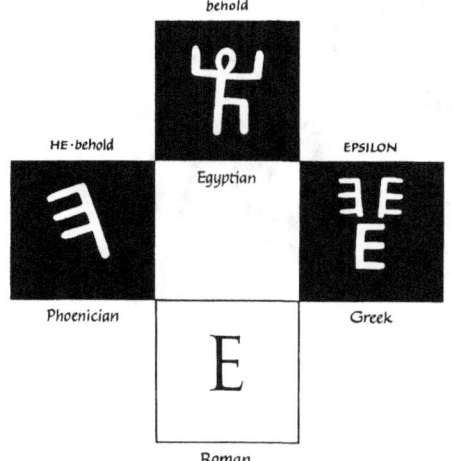

Egyptian hieroglyphs "behold"
Phoenician letter ⊒ name HE "behold"
Early Greek name EPSILON
Ⅎ RIGHT TO LEFT   E LEFT TO RIGHT
Early Roman E; Imperial Roman E

DEVELOPMENT OF LOWERCASE E

ẽ e e e e e
Rustic Uncial Half-Uncial Carolingian Gothic Humanist Italic

Ee Ee
Basic Italic Cursive Italic

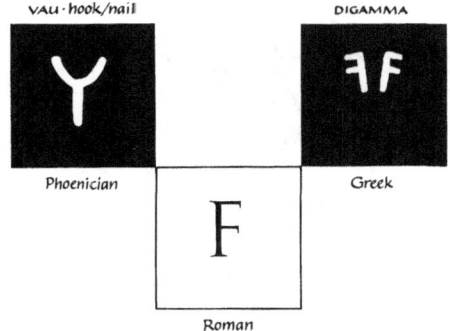

Phoenician letter Y name VAU "hook, nail"
Early Greek name DIGAMMA ꟻ RIGHT TO LEFT   F LEFT TO RIGHT
Early Roman F; Imperial Roman F

DEVELOPMENT OF LOWERCASE F

f F F f f f f
Rustic Uncial Half-Uncial Carolingian Gothic Humanist Italic

Ff Ff
Basic Italic Cursive Italic

TIMELINE

	EGYPTIAN	PHOENICIAN	EARLY GREEK	CLASSICAL GREEK / EARLY ROMAN / RUSTIC	IMPERIAL ROMAN / UNCIAL / HALF-UNCIAL	CAROLINGIAN / GOTHIC	ITALIC / HUMANIST
3000	2500	2000	1500	1000	500 BCE	0	500 CE	1000	1500	2000

Development of the Alphabet

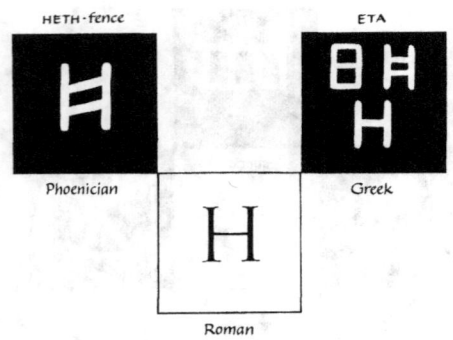

Phoenician letter ⊟ name CHETH "fence"
Early Greek name ETA ⊟ or ⊞
Classical Greek H
Early Roman H; Imperial Roman H

DEVELOPMENT OF LOWERCASE H

h h h h h h
Rustic Uncial Half-Uncial Carolingian Gothic Humanist Italic

Hh Hh
Basic Italic Cursive Italic

Egyptian hieroglyph ↷ "hand"
Phoenician letter ⌇
  name YOD "hand"
Early Greek name IOTA ⌇ RIGHT TO LEFT
ʃ LEFT TO RIGHT; Classical Greek I
Early Roman I
Imperial Roman I

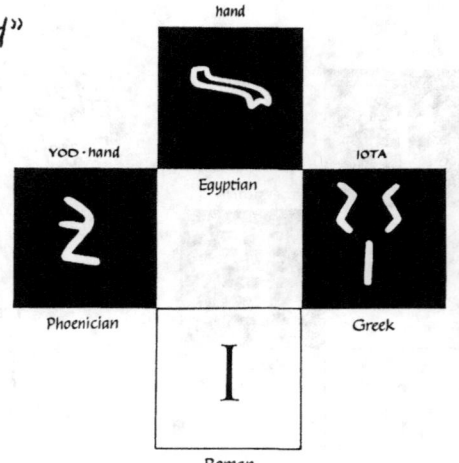

J is originally a variant of the letter I (long i). It was formally added to the alphabet in the 16th century.

DEVELOPMENT OF LOWERCASE I & J

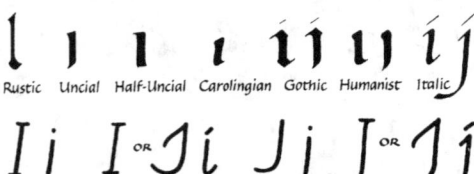
Rustic Uncial Half-Uncial Carolingian Gothic Humanist Italic

Ii   I or Ji   Jj   J or Jj
Basic Italic Cursive Italic Basic Italic Cursive Italic

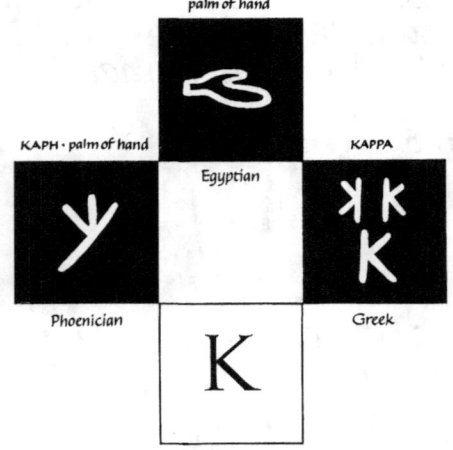

Egyptian hieroglyph ↶ "palm"
Phoenician letter Υ KAPH "palm"
Early Greek name KAPPA
  ꓘ RIGHT TO LEFT   K LEFT TO RIGHT; Classical Greek K
Early Roman K; Imperial Roman K
  K was rarely used.

DEVELOPMENT OF LOWERCASE K

K k k k k k
Rustic Uncial Half-Uncial Carolingian Gothic Humanist Italic

Kk or k   Kk
Basic Italic Cursive Italic

Development of the Alphabet

Egyptian hieroglyph ⌒ "ox goad, cudgel"
Phoenician letter ∠ name LAMED "ox goad, cudgel"
Early Greek name LAMBDA ⌐ or ⌐ RIGHT TO LEFT
Γ or L LEFT TO RIGHT; Classical Greek Λ
Early Roman L; Imperial Roman L

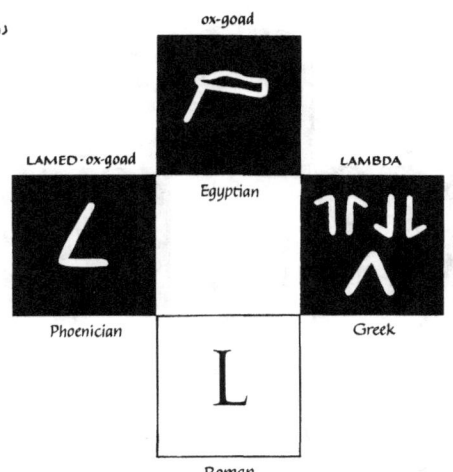

DEVELOPMENT OF LOWERCASE L

l l l l l l l
Rustic Uncial Half-Uncial Carolingian Gothic Humanist Italic

Ll Ll
Basic Italic Cursive Italic

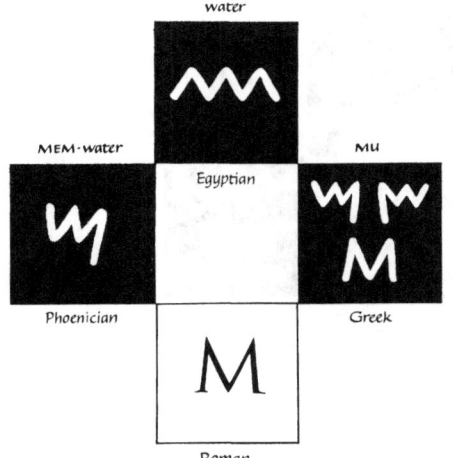

Egyptian hieroglyphs ∼∼∼ "water"
Phoenician letter ∽ name MEM "water"
Early Greek name MU ʍ RIGHT TO LEFT   M LEFT TO RIGHT
Classical Greek M
Early Roman M; Imperial Roman M

DEVELOPMENT OF LOWERCASE M

M m m m m m m
Rustic Uncial Half-Uncial Carolingian Gothic Humanist Italic

Mm Mm
Basic Italic Cursive Italic

Egyptian hieroglyph ⌒ "fish"
Phoenician letter ⌐ NUN "fish"
Early Greek name NU Ƴ RIGHT TO LEFT
N LEFT TO RIGHT; Classical Greek N
Early Roman N; Imperial N

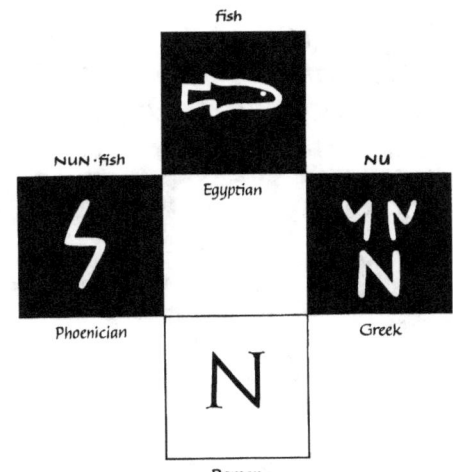

DEVELOPMENT OF LOWERCASE N

N N N n n n n
Rustic Uncial Half-Uncial Carolingian Gothic Humanist Italic

Nn Nn
Basic Italic Cursive Italic

Development of the Alphabet

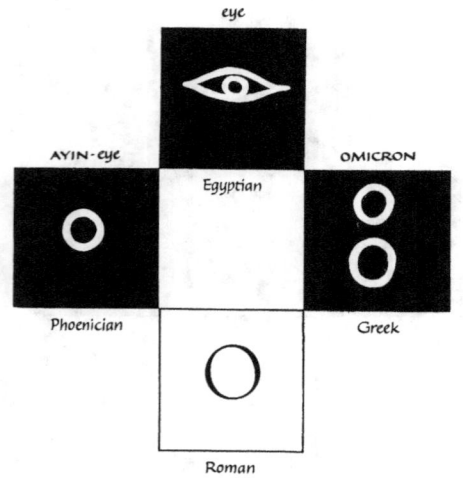

Egyptian hieroglyph 👁 "eye"
Phoenician letter o name AYIN "eye" (written smaller than others)
Early Greek name OMICRON, O
Classical Greek O
Early Roman O; Imperial Roman O

O has changed the least of all the letters since c. 2000 BCE.

DEVELOPMENT OF LOWERCASE O

O o o o o o O
Rustic Uncial Half-Uncial Carolingian Gothic Humanist Italic

Oo Oo
Basic Italic   Cursive Italic

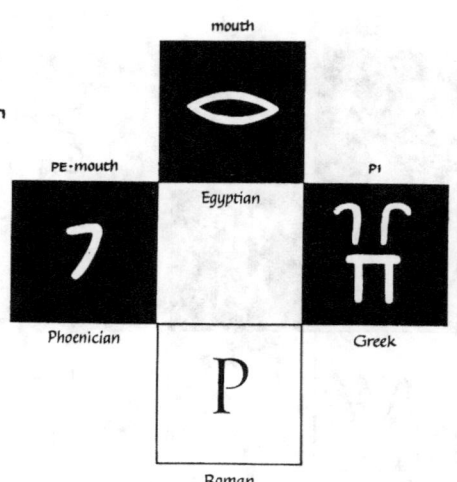

Egyptian hieroglyph ⌒ "mouth"
Phoenician letter ꎡ name PE "mouth"
Early Greek letter PI ꎡ RIGHT TO LEFT ꎡ LEFT TO RIGHT or ꎡ, ꎡ
Classical Greek Π
Early Roman Γ; Imperial Roman P

DEVELOPMENT OF LOWERCASE P

p p p p p p p
Rustic Uncial Half-Uncial Carolingian Gothic Humanist Italic

Pp Pp
Basic Italic   Cursive Italic

Phoenician letter ϙ name QOPH "knot"
Early Greek name KOPPA (Dropped from Classical Greek.)
Early Roman Q; Imperial Roman Q

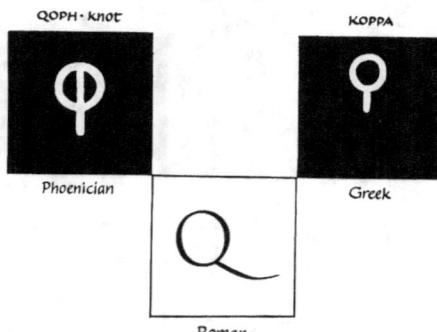

DEVELOPMENT OF LOWERCASE Q

Q q q q q q q
Rustic Uncial Half-Uncial Carolingian Gothic Humanist Italic

Qq Qq
Basic Italic   Cursive Italic

DEVELOPMENT OF OUR ALPHABET

Egyptian hieroglyph "head"
Phoenician letter ꟼ name RESH "head"
Early Greek letter RHO ꟼ RIGHT TO LEFT P LEFT TO RIGHT
Classical Greek P or P
Early Roman P R; Imperial Roman R

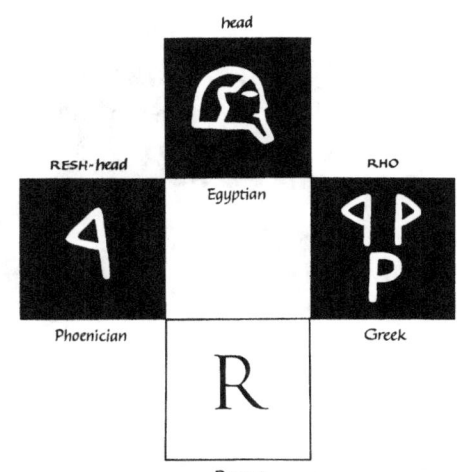

DEVELOPMENT OF LOWERCASE R

R r r r r r r
Rustic Uncial Half-Uncial Carolingian Gothic Humanist Italic

Rr Rr
Basic Italic   Cursive Italic

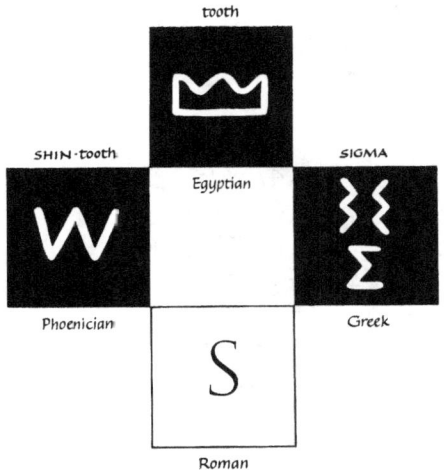

Egyptian hieroglyphs "tooth"
Phoenician letter W name SHIN "tooth"
Early Greek name SIGMA ⧸ RIGHT TO LEFT ⧹ LEFT TO RIGHT
Classical Greek Σ
Early Roman S; Imperial Roman S

DEVELOPMENT OF LOWERCASE S

S s ſ ſ ſs ſs ſs
Rustic Uncial Half-Uncial Carolingian Gothic Humanist Italic

Ss Ss
Basic Italic   Cursive Italic

Egyptian hieroglyphs ✛ X "mark"
Phoenician letter +, X name TAU "mark"
Early Greek name TAU T or T
Classical Greek T
Early Roman T; Imperial Roman T

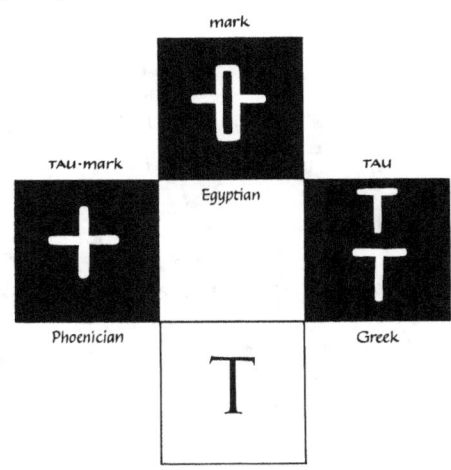

DEVELOPMENT OF LOWERCASE T

T T t t t t t
Rustic Uncial Half-Uncial Carolingian Gothic Humanist Italic

Tt Tt
Basic Italic   Cursive Italic

DEVELOPMENT OF OUR ALPHABET

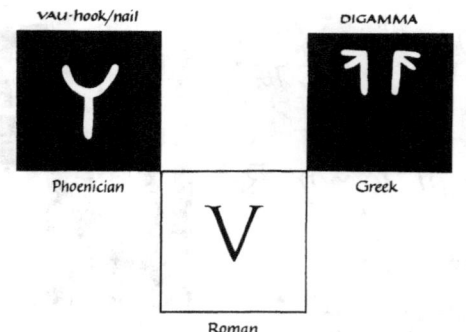

Phoenician letter Y name VAU "hook, nail"
Early Greek ⁊ RIGHT TO LEFT, Γ LEFT TO RIGHT
name DIGAMMA
Early Roman V; Imperial V

U *(16th c. form)*

U was the Medieval form of V. Both U and V were used interchangeably. In the 16th century U and V acquired their distinct pronunciations and U was formally added to the alphabet.

W *(16th c. form)*

W was invented by the Germanic people, c. 11th century, to distinguish a sound close to, but different from U. Two V's (U's) were linked together to form a new letter.

DEVELOPMENT OF LOWERCASE U, V, & W

V u u uu uvw uvw
Rustic Uncial Half-Uncial Carolingian Gothic Humanist Italic

Uu Uu Vv Vv Ww Ww
Basic Italic Cursive Italic Basic Italic Cursive Italic Basic Italic Cursive Italic

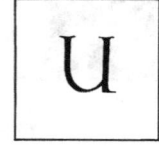

Phoenician letter ⟂ name SAMEKH "prop"
Early Greek Ξ or ⊞; Classical Greek: Ξ
Western X name XI; Eastern Ξ name XI
Early Roman X; Imperial Roman X

DEVELOPMENT OF LOWERCASE X

X x x x x x x
Rustic Uncial Half-Uncial Carolingian Gothic Humanist Italic

Xx Xx
Basic Italic Cursive Italic

Phoenician letter Y name VAU "hook, nail"
Early Greek Y (⁊⁊) DIGAMMA
Classical Greek Y UPSILON
Imperial Roman Y Added in the 1st century BCE to transliterate Greek words.

DEVELOPMENT OF LOWERCASE Y

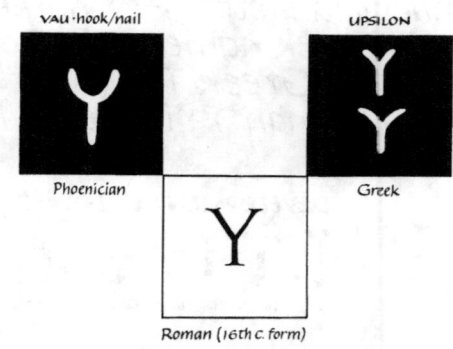

Y Υ γ v y yy
Rustic Uncial Half-Uncial Carolingian Gothic Humanist Italic

Yy Yy
Basic Italic Cursive Italic

Egyptian hieroglyph Z "sickle, weapon"
Phoenician letter Z name ZAYIN
    "sickle, weapon"
Early Greek I name ZETA
Classical Greek Z
Imperial Roman Z

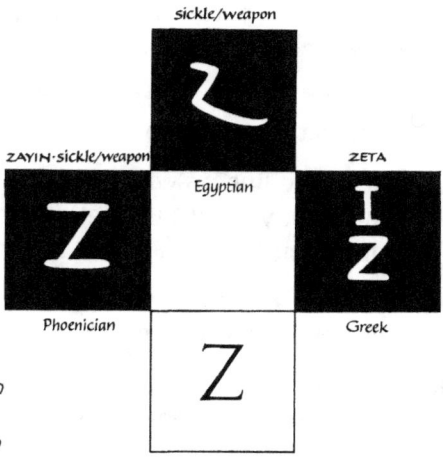

Z was added in the 1st century BCE to transliterate Greek words.

ZETA was the sixth letter of the Greek alphabet. It was not used in the Early Roman alphabet and its place was taken by G. When it was added, it went to the end of the alphabet.

DEVELOPMENT OF LOWERCASE Z

z z Z z ʒ Z Z
Rustic Uncial Half-Uncial Carolingian Gothic Humanist Italic

Zz Zz
Basic Italic Cursive Italic

IMPACT OF THE MAJOR HISTORICAL SCRIPTS

EGYPTIAN: Invention of the acrophonic principle — A picture of an object is used as a permanent representation for the initial letter of the word for the object.
2000 hieroglyphs of which 300 were common
Third millennium BCE to 1st century CE

PHOENICIAN: Creation of an alphabet using the acrophonic principle
22 letters
Second millennium BCE
☐, ⌐ came to represent the letter B because that is the first letter of the Semitic word for house—BETH.

GREEK: Addition of vowels — Many of the Greek names resemble the Phoenician names.
24 letters
Early: c. 1200 BCE to 400 BCE; Classical: c. 400 BCE to 100 CE
(aleph—alpha; beth—beta)

ROMAN: Dissemination of the alphabet throughout the Roman Empire
Early Roman: 21 letters; Imperial Roman: 23 letters
Early: 600 BCE to 30 BCE; Imperial: 30 BCE to 500 CE

RUSTIC: Flowing version of Roman capitals Roman; 30 BCE to 5th century CE

UNCIAL: Emerging ascenders and descenders Roman; 3rd to 9th centuries

HALF-UNCIAL: Lengthening ascenders and descenders Roman; 3rd to 9th centuries

CAROLINGIAN: Use of large size letters as capitals and small size letters as lowercase French, later international; 8th to 11th centuries

GOTHIC: Use of the same pen for capitals and lowercase European; 13th to 15th c.

HUMANIST: Combination of legible letters and a simplified writing procedure Italian; 15th to 16th centuries

ITALIC: Cursive version of Humanist Italian, English; 15th to 16th century

GLOSSARY

ASCENDER ▪ The part of a letter that extends above the waistline.

ARCH ▪ The part of a letter resembling an arch, such as the round portion of "n."

BASELINE ▪ The line on which letters "sit," bottom line of body height (sometimes called the writing line).

BASIC ITALIC ▪ A form of unjoined writing using italic letters without entrance or exit serifs.

BODY HEIGHT ▪ The distance between baseline and waistline (sometimes called "x" height).

BRANCHING LINE ▪ An imaginary line halfway between the baseline and waistline.

CALLIGRAPHY ▪ Beautiful or elegant writing, also the art of producing such writing. The letters are generally unjoined and often written with the edged tool. Italic calligraphy is one type of formal hand lettering or writing.

CAPITAL LETTER ▪ A letter in the series **A,B,C**, rather than **a,b,c** (sometimes called upper-case, large letters, or caps).

COUNTER ▪ Partially or fully enclosed space within a letter.

CROSSBAR ▪ A horizontal line, second stroke of **f** and **t**.

CURSIVE ITALIC ▪ A form of joined writing using italic letters with entrance and exit serifs. [Medieval Latin SCRIPTA CURSIVA - "Flowing script" - from Latin CURSUS, past participle of CURRERE - "to run."] Four characteristics of a cursive hand are elliptical forms, slight slope, fluent (mostly one-stroke letters), and joined letters.

DESCENDER ▪ The part of a letter that extends below the baseline.

DIAGONAL ▪ A line from lower left to upper right (as used in joins and letter shapes) or a line from upper left to lower right (as used in letter shapes).

DOWNSTROKE ▪ A line from top to bottom following letter slope angle.

ELLIPTICAL SHAPE ▪ A line following a compressed circular shape or elongated circle (as in *o*).

HORIZONTAL ▪ A line extending from left to right, parallel to baseline and waistline.

INTERSPACE ▪ An area between letters within words.

INVERTED ARCH ▪ The part of a letter resembling an upside-down arch such as "u."

ITALIC ▪ A script originating in Italy in the late 15th and early 16th centuries. It is characterized by slightly sloped, elliptical, fluent and often joined letterforms.

ITALIC HANDWRITING ▪ A system of writing for everyday use incorporating both an unjoined form of writing (basic italic) and a cursive form of writing (cursive italic).

JOT ▪ A short diagonal above i and j in place of a dot.

LETTER DIMENSIONS
  SHAPE ▪ The correct form of a capital or lower-case letter.
  SIZE ▪ The height and width of a letter.
  SLOPE ▪ The slant of a letter.
  SPACING ▪ The space between letters in words and space between words in a sentence.
  SPEED ▪ The rate of writing.

LOWERCASE LETTER ▪ A letter in the series **a, b, c**, rather than **A, B, C** (sometimes called small letters). [From the printer's practice of keeping the small letters in lower type cases or drawers.]

PEN EDGE ANGLE ▪ The angle of the edge of the pen nib in relation to the baseline.

SANS SERIF ▪ Without serifs, without any additions to the letter, as in basic italic.

SERIF ▪ An entrance or exit stroke of a letter.

STROKE ▪ Any straight or curved written line.

UPPERCASE ▪ See CAPITAL LETTER. [From the printer's practice of keeping the large letters in the upper type cases or drawers.]

WAISTLINE ▪ The top line of the body height.

BIBLIOGRAPHY

Anderson, Donna. "The Italic's Answer to Illegibility." *Vancouver Sun* (B.C.), February 21, 1976.

Bennett, Leslie, and Jack Simmons. *Children Making Books.* London: A&C Black Ltd., 1978.

Carter, Martha L. and Keith N. Schoville, editors. *Sign, Symbol, Script, An Exhibition on the Origins of Writing and the Alphabet.* Madison: University of Wisconsin, Madison, 1984.

Catich, Edward M., lecture at Reed College, Portland, Oregon, October 14, 1977.

———. *The Origin of the Serif.* Davenport, Iowa: The Catfish Press, St. Ambrose College, 1968.

Corballis, Michael C., and Ivan L. Beale. *The Psychology of Left and Right.* Hillsdale, N.J.: Lawrence Erlbaum Associates, 1976.

Cratty, Bryant J., *Developmental Sequences of Perceptual Motor Tasks: Movement Activities For Neurologically Handicapped and Retarded Children.* Palo Alto: Peek Publications, 1967.

Dubay, Inga and Barbara Getty. *Italic Letters: Calligraphy and Handwriting.* Portland, Oregon: Continuing Education Press, Portland State University, 1992.

Dubay, Inga. "The Write Stuff." Op-Ed. *The New York Times.* September 8, 2009.

———. *Getty-Dubay® Italic Calligraphy: for School & Home.* Portland, Oregon: Getty-Dubay Productions, 2016.

Edwards, Betty. *Drawing on the Right Side of the Brain.* Los Angeles: J.P. Tarcher, Inc., 1979.

———. *Drawing on the Artist Within.* New York: Simon & Schuster, 1986.

Fairbank, Alfred. *A Handwriting Manual.* New York: Watson-Guptil Publication, 1975.

———. *The Story of Handwriting.* New York: Watson-Guptil Publications, 1970.

Florey, Kitty Burns, *Script & Scribble: The Rise and Fall of Handwriting.* Brooklyn: Melville House Publishing, 2009, 2013.

Fry, Edward B., Dona Lee Fountoukidis, and Jacqueline Kress Polk. *The New Reading Teacher's Book of Lists.* New Jersey: Prentice Hall, 1985.

Gainer, William L., et al. *Observation Guide for the Santa Clara Inventory of Developmental Tasks.* Santa Clara: Zweig Associates, 1974.

Getty, Barbara. "A Case for Legibility." *The Oregon Elementary Principal.* (Fall, 1979): 19-20.

Getty, Barbara and Inga Dubay. *Getty-Dubay® Italic Handwriting Series (BOOKS A, B, C, D, E, F, G and INSTRUCTION MANUAL).* 4th ed. Portland, Oregon. Getty-Dubay® Productions, 2009-2013.

———. *Italic Handwriting Series (BOOKS A, B, C, D, E, F, G and INSTRUCTION MANUAL).* 3rd ed. Portland, Oregon. Continuing Education Press, Portland State University, 1994.

———. *Write Now: The Complete Program for Better Handwriting.* Portland, Oregon. Continuing Education Press, Portland State University. 1991, Rev. Ed., 2005.

———. *Write Now: The Getty-Dubay® Program for Handwriting Success.* Portland, Oregon. Getty-Dubay® Productions. 2011.

Gladstone, Kate. "Handwriting: The Perspective of a Survivor." *Their World* (a publication of the National Center for Learning Disabilities), no. 18. New York: 1995. 97-99.

———. Personal communication. May 19, 2013.

Glazer, Susan Mandel and Carol Smullen Brown. *Portfolios and Beyond: Collaborative Assessment in Reading and Writing.* Norwood, Massachusetts: Christopher-Gordon, Inc., 1993.

Groff, Patrick J. "Preference for Handwriting Styles by Big Business." *Elementary English*, no. 41 (December, 1964): 863-64, 868.

Herman, Joan L., Pamela R. Aschbacher, and Lynn Winters. *A Practical Guide To Alternative Assessment.* Alexandria, Virginia: Association for Supervision and Curriculum Development, 1992.

Herrick, Virgil E. "Comparison of Practices in Handwriting." *Childhood Education* 37 (February, 1961).

Jarman, Christopher J. *The Development of Handwriting Skills,* Great Britain: Basil Blackwell, 1979.

———. *Fun with Pens.* New York: Taplinger Publishing Co., 1979.

Kushki, Azadeh; Chau, Tom; Anagnostou, Evdokia. "Handwriting difficulties in children with autism spectrum disorders: a scoping review." *Journal of Autism and Developmental Disorders*, vol. 41, no. 12, December, 2011. 1806-16.

Bibliography

Lehman, Charles L., with contributing authors Donald Cowles and Gertrude Hildreth. *Handwriting Models for Schools*. Portland, Oregon: The Alcuin Press, 1976.

Lehman, Charles L., *Simple Italic Handwriting, A Teacher Guide for Grades 1–3*. New York: Pentalic, 1973.

Marano, Robert J. *A Different Kind of Classroom: Teaching with Dimensions of Learning*. Alexandria, Virginia: Association for Supervision and Curriculum Development, 1992.

Markham, Lynda R. "Influences of Handwriting Quality on Teacher Evaluation of Written Work," *American Educational Research Journal* 13, no. 4 (Fall, 1976): 277-283.

Mitchell, Ruth. *Testing For Learning: How New Approaches to Evaluation Can Improve American Schools*. New York: The Free Press, Macmillan, Inc., 1992.

Myers, Prue Wallace. "The Stages of Learning to Write," *The Journal of the Society for Italic Handwriting*, (Autumn, 1976): 88.

National Society for the Study of Education. *Education and the Brain*. Chicago: National Society for the Study of Education, 1978.

Neigebauer, Linda. A Statement Concerning Handwriting, an unpublished research paper, Portland, Oregon, 1973.

Palmer, Robert, et al. *Focusing on the Positive, Accommodating Students with Disabilities in Your College Classroom*. Portland, Oregon: Portland Community College, 1992.

Perrone, Vito, editor. *Expanding Student Assessment*. Alexandria, Virginia: ASCD, 1991.

Reynolds, Lloyd J. *Italic Calligraphy and Handwriting*. New York: Pentalic, 1969.

————. *Italic Handwriting* (from a report written at the request of the Oregon State Curriculum Committee), an unpublished paper. Portland, Oregon, 1969.

Sassoon, Rosemary. *HANDWRITING: The Way to Teach It*. Cheltenham, England: Stanley Thornes Ltd, 1990.

Schickedanz, Judith A. *More Than The ABCs: The Early Stages of Reading and Writing*. Washington, D.C.: National Association for the Education of Young Children, 1986.

Stewig, John. *Exploring Language Arts in the Elementary Classroom*, New York: CBS College Publishing, 1983.

Taylor, Stanford E., et al. *EDL Core Vocabularies in Reading, Mathematics, Science, and Social Studies*. New York: Educational Development Laboratories/ McGraw Hill, 1979. Source of graded vocabulary for BOOKS B-G.

Temple, Charles A., Ruth G. Nathan, and Nancy A. Burris. *The Beginnings of Writing*. Boston: Allyn and Bacon, Inc., 1982.

Ullman, B.L. *Ancient Writing and its Influence*. New York: Cooper Square Publishers, Inc. 1963.

Wallace, Don. "Sending The Right Message," *Success Magazine*, 62 (April 1989).

Getty-Dubay® Italic Handwriting Series Ruled Lines

Ruled Line Masters
Sample Letter Masters
Envelope Pattern

· abcdefghijklmnopqrstuvwxyz ·

Ruled Line Masters - 9mm (horizontal format)

Ruled Line Masters - 9mm

Name _____

1
2
3
4
5
6
7
8

This page may be reproduced for use with the *Getty-Dubay® Italic Handwriting Series*.
For inservice instruction, this page may be copied as projection transparency and/or teacher handout.

Ruled Line Masters - 6mm

Name

1.
2.
3.
4.
5.
6.
7.
8.
9.
10.
11.
12.

Ruled Line Masters - 6mm

Ruled Line Masters - 6mm with capital line

Ruled Line Masters - 5mm with capital line

Ruled Line Masters - 4mm with capital line

Ruled Line Masters - 9mm letter lines (horizontal format)

1 — date

2 — salutation

3 — body

4

5

6 — closing

7 — name

Place unlined sheet of paper over these lines when writing a rough draft or final copy of a letter.

This page may be reproduced for use with the Getty-Dubay® Italic Handwriting Series.

Getty-Dubay® Italic Handwriting Series · Instruction Manual

© 2012 Getty-Dubay® Italic Handwriting Series
available at www.handwritingsuccess.com

Ruled Line Masters - 6mm letter lines

street address

city, state, zip code

date

Dear
salutation

body

closing

your name (signature)

Place unlined sheet of paper over these lines when
writing a rough draft or final copy of a letter.

Ruled Line Masters - 5mm letter lines

Address

City, State

today's date.

Dear

Place unlined sheet of paper over these lines when writing a rough draft or final copy of a letter.

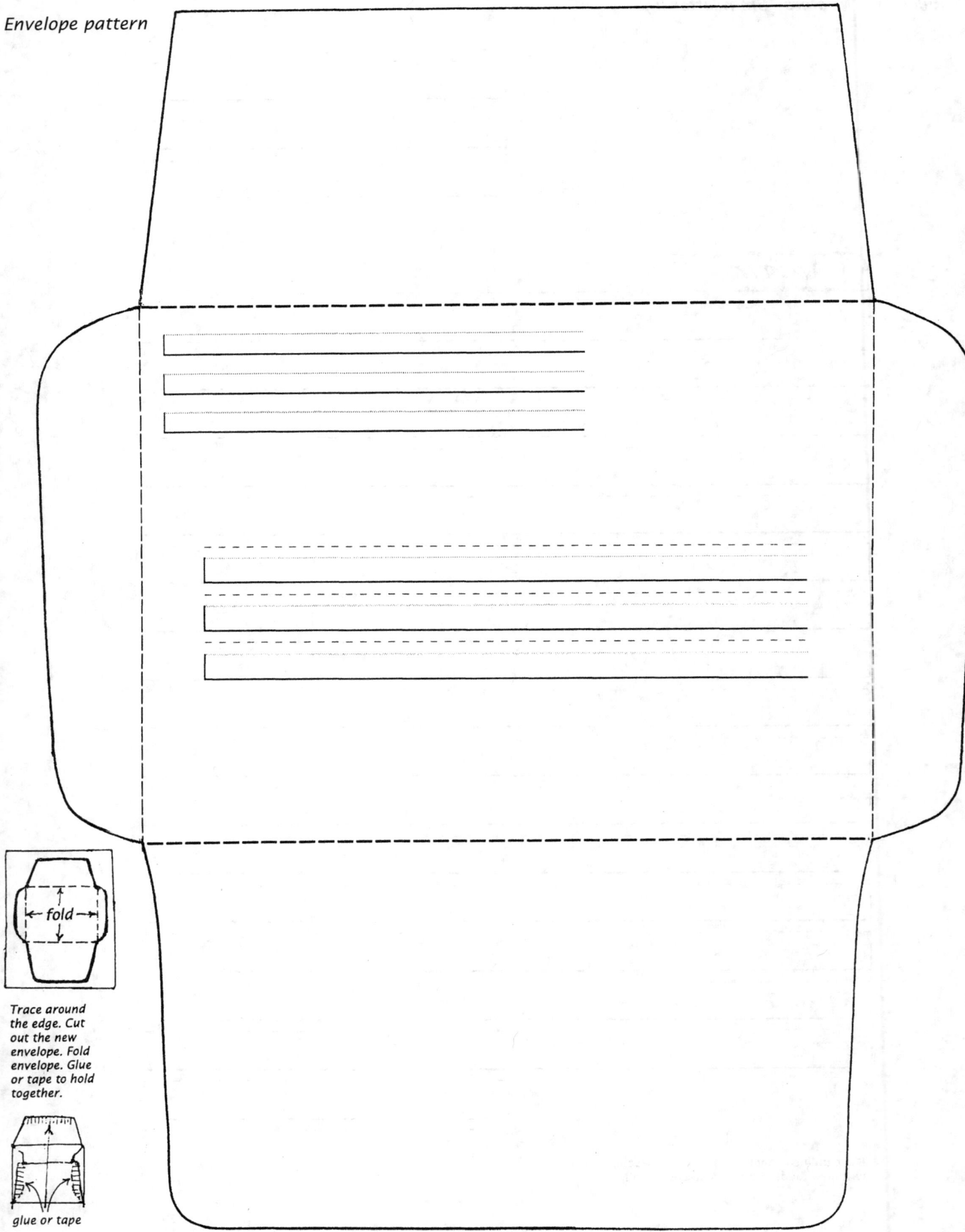

www.ingramcontent.com/pod-product-compliance
Lightning Source LLC
Chambersburg PA
CBHW051419070526
44584CB00023B/3492